CROSS COUNTRY AND ALL THE BULLSHIT WITH IT

Hood Lodo

ISBN-10: 1727002628

Dedicated to my daughter Amaris, who was just walking when I made this trip, and my daughter Ria, who was on her way to being born. If I die on my motorcycle before either of you can fully comprehend my love for you, I want to eternalize it right here in my words. If life ever makes you feel like an outcast, Daddy will always love and be with you in flesh or in spirit to help guide you. You both make me so proud.

Table of Contents

Prologue

I write this with a broken heart. Death has visited our nation every week for the past two months, ripping members away from this family. Funeral after funeral, we have come together to celebrate the lives of our fallen brothers. We share stories, we drink to memories, we teach each other of the men that are no longer with us. We comfort those who weep. We absorb animosity from the biological family who, sometimes, only know how to justify death with blame. We exhibit anger. We embrace each other with tight, mournful, bear-hugs. We kiss each other and exchange sentiments of love, underscored with the scent of whiskey on our breath. We laugh. Some cry. We commit to changes we swear to keep while in the moment. We are all confused. We unite, all loomed in the confusion cast by Death. It's a bittersweet celebration of our fallen brothers. We ride out and do our unique burial affairs under the guidance of our current national leader, who might not personally know the fallen, or who may. Then we mount up and ride back home to our respective states. We eventually sew on memorial patches commemorating our fallen. Some of us get tattoos. Some of us make memorabilia that we can keep in attempt to maintain the memories of those departed. We hunker down, retaliate, reorganize, ride, and then ride even more. Then, like an album on repeat play, we do it all over again. This is what the pattern is.

The one fact that will never change is that we will all die. We try to prepare. We make wills. We have insurance. We leave tools for our loved ones. We might even leave businesses or trust funds. We do what we think we should do during the time we do it in order to take care of what we need to as we know it. That's what we do, but is that enough? I mean, honestly, is that sufficient enough? Most of us are not famous. There might not be statues made or streets named after us when we are gone, but each of us has experiences that must also live on. We all have lived lives and are living lives that have extremely impactful events, challenges, successes, and failures that can grandly impact the people we love when we are gone. Some of us have children that we try to guide through mistakes we have made because of the wisdom we have gained through our own experiences. If only they knew that we made these experiences. If only they were able to know our individual stories. Some of our families forget the love we have for each other because they don't have the immediate reminders, like pictures, that show nothing but assistance to each other, smiles with one another, and love for one another. Many times, we get stuck in the last emotion we felt, which might be disdain. If only we took the time, somehow, to capture these moments and experiences so that they could be shared well after we are gone to assist those we love. If only we could show the methods to overcome some of the challenges we faced that could help, maybe, just one of the people we love after we are gone. If only our children could see, hear, or read about their prematurely-deceased parent firsthand. We struggle to learn people we love while they are alive, never mind when they are gone. It only makes sense, especially with the resources we have now, to capture our lives to the best of our abilities while we still can. It only makes sense to speak our individual stories, to the best of our abilities, firsthand. It only makes responsible sense to try to help whomever we can, however much we can, and enhance our legacy by capturing and sharing our stories so that they speak for us when we can no longer speak. Each of us are important factors in an amazing equation that can only be solved if we learn from one another. No matter how small, insignificant, grandiose, dark, embarrassing, humbling, or great your story is. It is your responsibility to those that love you to share it with them. So they can carry on...

For these reasons (along with popular demand from many of my bros), I release this story. It was written years ago during what some of those in our nation call "the honeymoon years". Those are the first five years in the club when you're bright-eyed and bushy-tailed. You're so in love with the club, and you think you know everything only to later realize that you don't know shit. You don't know shit about the club. You don't know shit about riding. You're learning. Sadly, many don't make it past five years. This is one of many stories I am choosing to now share with those that I love. Piece.

-Hood Lodo

HOOD LODO

Zero Day

It was supposed to be a carefree, freedom-spirited, all-American ride across the country. You know, the romantic shit you always think about: You and all your bros riding, with the roar of engines being the only sound heard. The wind is on your face as you ride in slow motion. You're an army of silhouettes with the sunset in front of you, proud and happy, without a worry in the world. It was supposed to be a ride decorated with plenty of stops at all the major landmarks and party destinations that our nation has to offer. It was supposed to be that type of trip that you would want to read about in, like, a book or something. Well, no dice. This was not that kind of trip, and this is not that kind of story. Pretty much like everything else related to the outlaw biker world: what you think it is going to be and how you think something is going to turn out is pretty much the one thing you can guarantee is *not* going to happen. My name is Hood, I'm an Outcast, and this is my story of my trip from the state of Massachusetts to the state of California and back and all the bullshit that happened in between. You might get something from it, you might not, but it's my story. It's our story.

It's not so much important to know who Outcast MC is but *what* Outcast MC is, and what it is not. For you to understand all this, I am going to have to run down a little bit about the motorcycle subculture, so bear with me. All this stuff you can find online, so I'm going to keep it simple. You have your independent riders who are people with motorcycles who have no affiliation to any organizations. Then you have groups that wear a one-piece back patch on their vests that says what riding club, social club, or veterans club they belong to. These groups are respected as riders, but since they do not exactly subscribe to the same rigors and structures as the subsequent tiers, they are generally not really involved or viewed as Motorcycle Clubs (MCs). MCs are clubs that subscribe to the structure of affiliations and territories that make up much of this subculture or what is now known as "the set". They wear two-piece back patches that may have their name on the top merged with a center image and then a separate bottom rocker that declares what city or town they represent. They get "blessed off" or are granted access to being part of a network of affiliations by a dominant club. Dominant clubs are typically "outlaw" clubs, which are distinguished by three separate patches on their vests and go through rigorous challenges to earn the right to wear each of these patches. (Note that "outlaw" clubs are a tier of the motorcycle hierarchy, and when referred to as such it is not to be confused with The Outlaws MC, which is the name of a specific outlaw club as well.) The top rocker is their club name, which is separated *completely* from their center logo. This is also completely separate from their bottom rocker, which indicates their state spelled out in its entirety, denoting that they have control of regions in that state. Amongst these outlaw clubs are the very top tier organizations, which are the "1%ers" or clubs that award the 1%er diamond patch. I must stress the level of significance these top tier organizations have. They have decades of history. Most of them have origins from soldiers who have served in historical wars and take the concept of brotherhood directly from combat. They have exclusive membership and fierce value systems. Bottom line is these are the no-bullshit clubs that control the entire motorcycle subculture. These are the motherfuckers your favorite TV shows are based on. Here is where I will introduce Outcast MC. We are the only all black, traditional outlaw 1%er club in the world. We have chapters in damn near every state in United States, and our history extends back close to half a century. For now, this is all I'm going to share about the history of this club. The rest you are going to have to find out by speaking directly to members of your local Outcast MC face to face.

There is one thing you better be willing and ready to do being in Outcast MC, and that's ride your shit. Members in this club ride for real. Our calendar is jam-packed with events across the nation. Some events are mandatory and being on iron is obviously expected. I come from a chapter that has bros that have ridden from Boston, Massachusetts to Alaska. I am surrounded by bikers in my state that wear a state-made "100,000 miles" patch, which signifies them putting in 100,000 Outcast-miles on one bike. They don't brag about that shit or talk too much about riding, because it is expected. Riding your iron is what is the basis behind building any of the bonds that are going to form from being in an outlaw club. It's not about the destination or about the distance. It's about the ride. It's about the stories that come from the ride. Stories that will cause bros to argue about what really happened. Stories that will get bros nicknames they won't be able to shake for life. Stories that identify who the bros are that stand solid in a fucked-up situation, and who are not. Stories that declare what kind of biker you are. Do you crumble and whimper like a little bitch when things get rough, or do you suck it up and drive on? Do you run towards the fight, or from the fight when shit pops off? The truth is going to come out, and the road is going to expose it. I learned a lot of things about myself and about Outcast during this trip. Some are good. Some are fucked up. All of them are true.

One of our national events fell in California this year. So, this was a perfect opportunity for the conversation of a cross-country chapter ride to come up. A few of us were lightly speaking it all through a few months earlier at the clubhouse to get ideas on how we wanted to approach it. We agreed we wanted to see some sites and shit and visit bros at various Outcast clubhouses on the

7

way. We were speaking about taking a good two weeks off to commit to the trip.

After that, the cross-country trip conversation would come up sporadically some nights at the clubhouse, but not often. It didn't seem like many bros were going. I already had it locked in my mind that I was going, so that was that. If you have ever planned the movement of any group before, you know that it can look good on paper, but the day of execution is the only thing that matters. That's when you see who actually is showing up and who isn't. One thing that is a peeve of mine is last minute fall-outs or any other flakey shit like that. If you say you are going to be somewhere, then be there. Other than that, just say, straight-out, that you are not going. Many bros flat-out said no they could not make a trip like that this year. Some were trying to feel out who else was going. I made my mind up I was going. Because I decided to commit to this ride, I had sacrificed a lot of other rides with the group in my endless balancing act of life with Outcast. There was something different about this ride. Something that made it more important to me than any other ride. Just the idea of embarking on this mission was activating something familiar that had been dormant for a while. It was activating a side of me that had not needed a home since I last returned to the United States from war a few years back.

In Outcast you have to earn your biker name. You receive it when you finally get patched over – however many years or months that takes. The name is part of your rebirth into this new organization and should, in my opinion, be directly and strictly related to experiences you have created with your bros as an Outcast. I don't think anyone should be given a name they carried on from somewhere else. I have earned the name Hood in Outcast. I have also earned quite a few names in quite a few other walks of my life. One of them is Night Wolf, which is a name earned by being part of a very coveted sixteen soldier team in the Army known as Wolf Pack, while in Afghanistan.

I have done a few tours in a few places in the Middle East and East Asia, but for now, I will focus on my last one where the Wolf Pack was birthed. I did a couple of tours in the very early stages of Operation Iraqi Freedom, so I will bring up a little bit about my second one as well. I was part of a small group that was out in the streets pretty fucking heavily, nicknamed "The Patriot Element". I guess you can say I've dealt with battle. That's not a glorification or a simplification. It's just something I want known so that you can understand the experiences that lead up to all this cross-country shit and this outlaw motorcycle club shit as a whole.

Both in Iraq and in Afghanistan, I was out there very heavily in the streets. I was involved. *We* were involved. I have seen a lot of blood and have done a lot of things and have reflected a lot on war. I'm not getting into all of it here. And I don't get all into it in person, because I have come to a resolve that the only people that my experiences in those tours of war genuinely matter to is The Patriot Element and The Wolf Pack. That's it. I don't typically care to do the whole "war stories" thing and trade stories with other soldiers who ask about deployments. A lot of soldiers really don't ask questions with the intention of learning or bonding with anything; they mostly just ask you questions to compare it to their experiences if they were deployed before, or to try and match it up to whatever their far-fetched understandings of war are if they have not. Validation is what I call it. Ultimately, I couldn't care less about either. I used to get into comparing stories and speaking all about shit, but now I just listen to people ramble about their experiences. I don't share. I don't wear some medals sometimes. Other times I do. I just don't care anymore for all the fanfare behind war. I've processed enough, have dealt with enough, and have partitioned the experiences in a manner that is far more important than the validations most seek from speaking their war stories. You already got the simple, stupid answers most of you are looking for. Have I seen shit? Yes. Have we lost people and all that crap? Yes. The more important topic I want to speak on is how war has changed me. Because, unknown to me at the time, a portion of that change has a lot to do with what made me seek Outcast in the first place.

I guess, somehow, and there is no other way to put it, all my deployments, especially the last one, kind of fucked me up a little. Not terribly. I wouldn't even say completely in a bad way. It just changed me. Seeing so much shit and processing so much death kind of put a new perspective on life. It, ultimately, just made me genuinely not give a fuck about a lot of shit, because it made me hyper focus on the more important aspects of life. So much so that a lot of people's normal activities and ideas seemed very trivial to me. So I simply cut everyone off. Like, everyone on Facebook and all that shit. I completely couldn't tolerate reading about the superficial bullshit anymore. I couldn't give a fuck about what the hell was happening at such and such club on "Whip-em-out Wednesday", "Thirsty Thursday", "Freaky Friday" or whatever the fuck lame-ass status someone was crying about in my news feed. The shit became repulsive to read because I felt distant from all of that. I was still thinking about Rob getting blown up by a vest of eight grenades at the gate in Phoenix from a suicide-bomber dressed like the Afghan National Army. Only two of the eight went off, but it was enough to kill him. He was a young soldier. A kid who had a kid. A little girl. I was one of the riflemen that fired in his 21-gun salute. I'm communicating with his family (not that I knew him, or his family that well) in between silly fucking messages telling me I got tagged in some fucking shoe ad, or dickheads inviting me to play some stupid game app, or some fuck-face I don't know

10

telling me to listen to their mixtape. Go fuck yourself with a curling iron, seriously! I just felt completely disconnected from people when I got home. I was numb to all the silly shit. My circle got real small, real quick, and I only gave energy to people whom I felt loved me genuinely. The type of love you can feel. I was sensitive to that, which made me very aware of it. Being out and doing social bullshit was not for me anymore. My patience was non-existent, because I just didn't feel like anyone really qualified for me to fake like I gave a fuck about whatever nonsense with which they were about to waste my time. So I'd rather remove myself from the bullshit than really hurt motherfuckers' feelings. It wasn't anger. It was just a real cold, no-fuck-giving me. Like, *Yeah, so you did bla bla bla? Why the fuck are you telling me this? What the fuck is your point? Ask me for whatever favor you're about to ask me for so I can tell you to go fuck off because you're not my kid.* I was like that.

I understood this to be a temporary, transitional phase back into the life I used to know and live. Something similar happened when I returned from my earlier tours in Iraq. But, this time was different. I stayed like that. It seemed like a permanent change. I say it was not bad because, in all honesty, the people who I was like that with could fuck off. We might call ourselves friends or have socialized forever, but my definition of friendship changed because of war. My definition of everything changed because of war. I had more of a connection in a year with people that have been through some crazy shit with me than people with whom I spent most of my life doing superficial shit. At this point, I don't know if that's actually true, but that's how I felt at the time, because that is what was real at the time. I still felt those experiences. So, I felt connected to only those who experienced them with me. I came fresh back from war, and it's like I never left. The people I dealt with before I left had the same problems and were talking about the same bullshit when I came back. To

11

me, it was like they got stuck in time, and I got catapulted ten years forward. They say you age ten years at war. Well, they used to say that. I hope that's not true, but I think the point is your perspective gets real mature, real quick. You get weathered and over-stimulated.

I had several roles in Afghanistan. One was the QRF (Quick Reaction Force) commander. I'm going to try and stay away from all the military jargon and acronyms, but you are going to have to learn a few to grasp the context. QRF is the assault team the base sends out to rapidly respond to any combat, emergency, or developing situation. If there is a firefight, and the ground force needs backup, QRF responds. If a blast happens, QRF responds and secures the site until all the other forces come in. QRF might have to create a landing zone for the choppers to come in and extract the wounded. Whatever it may be, QRF has to be on top of all the forces on the ground and know where they are in the area so that we can readily respond if needed.

This was one of several missions Wolf Pack acquired. We became familiar with the streets of Afghanistan, so we were constantly asked to pick up personnel and do other logistic missions. We were not anything special, just normal ground troops, but we grew close and tight. We went through a lot together. I still can smell the scent of the burnt soldiers whose bodies were fused to their SUV seats that we pulled out of their vehicles on the day I now just call "May 18th". I remember Grey Wolf's face when he saw all their gear melted into their flesh. I remember Vespa Wolf and I picking up body parts for what seemed like forever. It was one of the biggest blasts in the history of Kabul at the time. Over a ton and a half of explosives packed in a vehicle-borne IED that destroyed a whole convoy and a dozen other vehicles. The targeted eighteen were dead and fifty-seven were wounded including civilians. The death toll undoubtedly was going to go up, because those evacuated from the scene surely died in transit to whatever medical facility they went. We were out there trying to collect all the dead up. It took so long because the blast scattered body parts and debris in over a two-hundred-meter radius. We filled every cadaver bag out of our mortuary kits, which we kept in each gun truck. We reverted to wrapping our comrades' body parts up in blankets and anything else we could find to transport them in the backs of our assault vehicles. It was so fucking hot you could feel the death mixed in with the heat and smog. I would crouch down, peer across the ground, and watch for a collection of small flies swarming around to indicate to me where human flesh was. Then I would go collect it. For some reason *that* just felt like the most important fucking thing for us to do in that moment. We had already secured the perimeter and had the scene locked in, but now it was collecting every piece of the dead up, because we were not leaving one fragment of our dead in those fucking streets. I still hear Sneaky Wolf's voice in my head coming through our vic-system headset saying, "There's dead bodies everywhere, bro." He was my gunner so when our gun truck pulled up he was the first in my truck to be able to see the whole scope of the blast from up there. Mangled vehicles were everywhere...Ok, I'm cutting this story off here.

I swear I could write six books with the shit I have stored in my head from war, good and bad. But I bring all that shit up because I'm trying to get you to understand the changes that happened and why they happened. Those people I went through that shit with, those people who were on CNN and in The Boston Herald and all that shit with me. Those people who, before we even got back to base the media had images and video of us blasted all over Al Jazeera and the internet, whose families knew the story and were terrified at home before the military could even make up a lie. Those people are the only people I really felt connected to besides the very few family members and even fewer friends that contributed from back home to our existence out there at war. That pocket was very small. I felt very connected to them, and those are the only people I chose to surround myself with for a long time. It felt right. I didn't fuck with civilians. I stayed to myself and my family. I didn't socialize online. My cell phone, which used to be glued to my ear with the dozens of people I interacted with from sun up to sun down, didn't even get picked up. It would ring, and I would just not answer it. I rolled out by myself, who knows where sometimes, just to think. It was liberating to not give a fuck about all the senseless shit I used to give a fuck about before. I am able to explain this now, in retrospect, but when it was going on, I didn't realize how I was acting. It was not really apparent to me that I had turned into an outcast before I turned into an Outcast.

I have quite a range, as far as experiences, in my deployments. I have led troops, I have been led by troops. I have been kinetic in the streets, and I have had my endurance tested in guard towers of holding camps. I have laughed, and I have shed tears. I've thought I was going to die, and I have lived. That level of living is hard to come down from. Once you have broken through to that type of constant stimulation every day, it becomes damn near a subtle addiction that takes over your being. You can't really go backward after that. So, I'm home with this very clear way of thinking: Fuck off unless you directly contribute to my development and my life. Go juggle hand-grenades if you're a ball of negative energy or someone who just wants to cry like a little bitch all the time.

I'm also very well versed in weapons but just didn't feel like I had a fucking home for this skill or the others mentioned while back here in the States. I either go back to war, which I definitely was not going to volunteer to do, or I inadvertently compensate. The latter is what ultimately happened.

14

Long story short, I got exposed to the motorcycle set. After having a bunch of 99% clubs explore me, and me them, I realized a new dawn was about to happen for me. I started exploring Outcast and I knew, hands down, that this was going to be the road I was going to walk. I stalked Outcast and that alone started to stoke the fires I am used to. The organization is very shadowy. It's not a flashy club at all. In fact, it's the exact opposite. It's an extremely rugged group. It is difficult to get information on, and it is something you will never really understand unless you walk the path. It is the dark-side, the night. So naturally, Night Wolf was on it. The hunt began, and after a long and tedious journey, the results became what they were going to ultimately become the minute I set my sights on this club. I earned the right to wear the words Outcast across my shoulder blades and carry our coveted symbol, "The Old Man", on my back. I won't speak on the process because that's not what we do, but I will reiterate that we *earn* our shit. If it's not earned, then there is no pride in it. If there is no pride in it, then it won't be done right. I became an Outcast, and I was revitalized. It definitely is not Wolf Pack. It definitely is not Patriot Element. But neither of those groups are Outcast. The club named me Hood. The National President's meeting, in Long Beach, California, was the first ride I was about to take that felt like a mission. So, I treated it like one.

The "Cali Plan", was that there was no plan. Three Piece (the name of the road captain at the time) and I had light conversation at the clubhouse about what we wanted to do as far as Cali went. We both agreed we wanted to take a moderate pace and have the capabilities of stopping and seeing the Grand Canyon. Maybe, working into the plan some days in Las Vegas and all that kind of stuff. We invited input from Grasshopper, a founder of our chapter and national vice-president at the time, who really left the plan up to those going. Grass has made trips like this

15

several times and I think he was leaving the lane open for whomever was going to write their own destiny. I had spoken to Magnum, another founder of our chapter, to get his input. It was really just up to Three Piece, as the road captain, and the bros going to dictate what they wanted to do.

So as time got closer and no one really laid out a solid plan of what the route was going to be, things started to look a little shaky. I met Three Piece at the clubhouse one night and asked him, "What's up with Cali, and what's our route?" Three looked back at me, curled his mouth up in that weird, smiley, smirky way he does whenever he talks and said, "Man, I'm just gonna wing it!" I fucking burst out laughing, slapped him on the back and said, "That's what the fuck it is then. Good!" Fuck it. That was magic to my ears because... I don't really know why, but it was. I guess it was just more realistic than him making up a bunch of shit to sound like he knew what he was doing. He never made this trip before either. We knew we were heading west. The rest was unwritten. I was game. Fuck it.

I recall asking Patches, the Sergeant at Arms at the time, if he was going and him responding with, "Shit, I'm going, are you going is the question?" There really hadn't been much communication with me about the trip for a while, and my military schedule seems to conflict perfectly with damn near everything related to Cast. The last church meeting we had, the Cali trip was discussed. Bros got an idea of who was going from that. Since I was not there (again at military training) maybe there was question on whether or not I was rolling. "Hell yeah, I'm rolling!" was my response to Patches, and I couldn't be more sure of this. When I say shit, I mean it. If I say I'm going to be somewhere, I'm there. If I say I'm going to do something, it's done. At this point the bros going are as follows: Three (RC), Grass (National VP), Patches (SAA), Shooter (Chapter President), and Hood (soldier). There are still some bros uncertain if they are going; these are the bros definitely going. Grass is expecting his granddaughter to be born a day after we leave so he might have to catch up to the pack. The plan is to leave on Saturday, and as long as we all are in position by the following Saturday, which is the meeting, then all is good. As I stated earlier, fucking with outlaws, "the plan" is the one thing you can guarantee is *not* going to happen.

I've been getting my iron set for this trip and making sure everything is squared away. I ordered brand new saddlebags, because I went down on my bike not too long ago and shredded the bags I had. I banged the bike up, but I did the repairs and got her back to operational. I replaced the fuel tank and gauges with parts I purchased on eBay. I replaced the clutch master-cylinder, left side mirror, passenger foot peg, and ordered new lights. I changed out the left grip and installed a windshield on her. She did not have one, and I figured Cali would be the trip to try one out. I installed a phone cradle for GPS, and a dedicated USB/cigarette-lighter power source. For extra storage, I ordered a medium-sized, magnetic tank bag that lay right on the fuel tank. I was pretty confident with this setup.

"Breakout" is a club's annual reintroduction into the motorcycle scene for the year. It is when all the bikes must be 100% operational and is when the club presents themselves with all their support clubs and the likes. Typically, there is a power run somewhere then a big party at the clubhouse. Our breakout run was a week before the trip. Everything was good on the bike for breakout, but my tires were a little too worn for my peace of mind as far as the Cali trip. I figured during the week I would get my tires replaced. No big deal, right? Well, apparently every swinging dick in the region is getting their fucking bikes worked on at the same time. It's the beginning of riding season so the usual-suspect places to get maintenance done are mobbed. I mean they are pushed back with appointments for months! The shit's ridiculous. I'm calling everywhere to find some fucking tires, and I'm coming up with nothing. I'm telling shops I'm going cross-country on *Saturday* and they are like, "Ok Mr. Hood, so, yeah, let's set it up for *Monday*, and we can have you all taken care of." I do believe I just said I was leaving on Saturday. What the fuck? Are they on some Mayan calendar shit, or something, because I'm pretty sure Monday doesn't sound like Saturday? Not only is it impossible to get a place that can do the installation, but I need tires too. So, I might find a place with an opening, but they don't have my tires and can't get them until whenever. I started calling out of state. I know if I order the tires online they are not going to come in time. So I'm at it. I even start tapping into my military network and working that angle. Dudes all over the place are like, "Hell yeah. I got a tire place." They can do it all up for cheap too, but the time was the only issue. So I'm scrambling. Not to mention, I find out my fucking iron has some strange-ass setup as far as its tires go. Words of wisdom when changing tires: Never Google search or go off spec sheets and shit about what size tires your bike has. Go directly to the tire that is on it and get the dimensions directly off there. Get the make of those tires too, because that makes a difference on how they are installed. Pay attention to the load bearing code as well. You might have the right size tire but the weight for which it is rated does not fit the weight of your bike. This was the exact situation I was facing with my iron.

I think I might take this moment to introduce you to the iron that I'm working with. We are speaking about the 2004 Suzuki VZ1600 Marauder. The bike is a power cruiser (similar in posture to the Harley Davidson V-Rod Muscle I ride now). Well, this bike happens to have race bike sized tires but, weighing in at something like 700lbs, it needs street bike tires with a higher load capacity. So, I'm scrambling to try and get some tires, and everyone is saying they can't help me. I ended up rush ordering, on a

Thursday night, tires that even with rush ordering were not going to arrive until Monday. I texted Three and Patches to let them know what's going on. They inform me of some plan changes that might work out in my favor. Shooter is planning on rolling out with Grass now, whenever his granddaughter is born, as opposed to with the main group.

So, again, the main body is rolling out on Saturday. My tires are scheduled to come in on Monday. I texted Grass to see what's up with him and his granddaughter, and as of that Thursday she had not been born. I checked up on Grass the next day to see if she was born yet, and he responded with a text saying, "Bro, if you wait on me you might not be going." I respond with, "I'm not waiting on you, brother, just asking about you. My tires are in Monday, and I'm hard pushing out that day. Three is maintaining contact with me and letting me know his checkpoints. Once my tires are good I'm rolling. I'm rocking, solo or not." The destination is to be in Long Beach on Saturday, May 24th. It's Sunday, "May 18th", and I'm already a day behind the group. No matter, I have already started to get that silent calm that settles in when you know you are about to trek out on your own. In my mind, the idea of catching the pack is not ideal, and as time continues I'm unsure if it is even going to be my plan. I'm forging my own way on this one. The first group shot to New Jersey for an event then pushed from there. I missed that event, so I re-adjusted my direction and pointed my sites at Detroit. So, at this point it was decided that my whole journey was going to be different. I was not going to catch up with the pack. I was moving in my own lane. That's just how it was going to go down.

Lone Wolf style is how I was going to handle this. Lone Wolf is one of my closest brothers in the Wolf Pack. We have been through it all together in Afghanistan. He would always stray from the pack and be out there fucking with the Afghans. He was named Lone Wolf for that. We would be over here plotting some shit, or whatever, and

19

HOOD LODO

Lone Wolf would have his boots off in some fucking hut, on some rug, drinking tea with some Afghan, laughing and shit. Neither one of them would know what the other was saying but they didn't need to. Then his Puerto Rican accent would fly out from the hut, "Night Wolf, come here Pa-Pa! Taste this tea, ja ja ja! It tastes like shit, bro!" Then I'd be over there by his side drinking some nasty-ass tea.

My brigade is going to the Joint Readiness Training Center in Louisiana. Every time we train at JRTC we end up getting deployed. They are not saying we are going to war again, but you kind of only go to this place and train to this degree when you are getting ready to go to war. I say that because my military schedule and my Outcast schedule compete with each other. So in that spirit, the preparation for the climactic training that I am going to attend lines up with this climactic cross-country trip I'm about to take. My military gear has to get shipped out weeks before I actually fly out to the training site. So, I am at home packing for both California with Outcast and Louisiana with the military at the same time. I put gear in my rucksack then put gear in my saddlebags. I don't mean to make it such a dramatic process, with a bunch of piles of gear all over the living room, but I do. I make a packing list in my notepad, detailing where I have placed everything as I pack. It has become habitual for me. I always pack at the last minute. It's just my pattern. I have done this countless times. I am always packing for something. If it's not some training for this, it's some training for that. I do a lot, and I reiterate *a lot*, of specialized training. I can whip a rucksack together for weeks of training in short time.

I've never packed for long distance riding though. In fact, I'm just getting used to the luxury of having saddle-bags. I never cared for them before. My bike is simple. It has no radio, no front fairing, no ape-hanger handlebars. I recently put a windshield on her. There are not many comfort commodities on her at all. Similarly, when I pack for training, I never bring some of the other comfort items other troops bring like pillows and blankets and shit. I bring the bare minimum for survival. It's almost senseless how much I disregard comfort. I have been in absolutely terrible conditions that could have been significantly changed with the simplest of comfort items, but I don't calculate these things as necessary many times. I'm unsure why I'm like that, but I guess the benefit is that it has made me a durable person. It's aided me in being mentally tough. At least that is what I tell myself. Mental toughness is as important, and arguably more important, than physical toughness. I can't stress that enough. That is going to play into this trip heavily. I just don't know it yet.

It's Sunday morning and calm. I have a New Jersey chapter soft colors hooded sweatshirt on. (Soft colors are the same three patch design that is on your vest but on a shirt or sweatshirt. It is exclusively worn by a member of the club and treated very much like a vest but not exactly to that degree.) Let me tell you, the NJ hoodie is one of the best hoodies I have ever had. If you are an Outcast and you don't have a New Jersey chapter hoodie, you need to get one! It's definitely one of my most used Outcast items to date. I crack a beer from the fridge and say to my very pregnant wife (she is eight months pregnant with my second daughter at this point), "We should go get breakfast." She agrees. It's not something we typically do, but it's just that type of day. We gather up my one-and-a-half-year-old daughter, and we go to this spot not too far from the house. It's a little home-cooking, rustic style breakfast spot. I've learned to appreciate these types of places. I'm not a food chain style of dude. I like little secret coves that serve good food on old plates. Those types of places that have that old lady in there looking confusingly at the cash register as she slowly pokes away at the complicated "do-hicky". In any other job she would be fired. It's ok because you never are at these places when

21

you're in a hurry. I have my youth in my arms as we walk inside. My wife already knows that I select the seating position that has the best vantage point and a couple of other factors that she has just learned over time dealing with me. She knows that I will not have my back to certain scenarios, so her pausing for a moment, for the result of my brief calculations is automatic. We are seated perfectly, enjoying the ambiance and our daughter with her antics.

Even in daddy mode with my daughter, who commands so much attention, I am aware of my sur-roundings. Maybe even more so when I'm with my daughter. I notice each person and assess how much of a threat they are. I have always done this. I take note of all the people who enter the place. I notice this one guy come in, and he has tattoos all over him. He has tats on his face and head and all. He has a calmness to him. His whole style screams *biker*. He is with whom appears to be his ol' lady and kids. It's ironic, 'cause I'm used to being the sore thumb in many environments, even when I am extremely reserved. Sometimes, by just being the only black person in an area. I stand out many times. It was interesting to have another element in this wholesome environment that commanded that much attention as well. It's also amazing how much having children around you and being "Daddy" pacifies one's image. I swear you could roll up and knock the president off if you have a cute little baby with you. The baby has to have a certain character though, not any baby can pacify an audience. My daughter has that unique charm. She can bring the cupcake out of everyone. It's senseless to resist it. The damn kid is hilarious and adorable. The dude, who I suspect is a biker, escorts who appears to be his son into the bathroom. As they pass me, I hear them talking about whatever nine-year-olds talk about. Moments later, the duo come back out from the bathroom. The kid pushes forward, and the biker-looking dude pauses behind me for a moment and says, "Outcast? Hey, how you doing?" and extends his hand. "I'm Monster, Regional

Vice President of The Outlaws." I introduce myself, "Hood, Outcast Massachusetts." We shake hands. We continue talking, lightly, about things we talked about. It was peaceful. I was just with the Massachusetts chapter president of The Outlaws a few days ago at our breakout party. There was a mutual respect for the other's organization, an understanding of the setting we were in, and the civilians we were both with. He was with his family, and I was with mine. From the outside looking in, with the big smiles, wide eyes, and courtesy shown by both parties, you would think we were military buddies or something. We talked as if we were alumni at a reunion, but no. We are just both bikers in outlaw men's clubs. There is a respect shown to that alone. Outcast MC is a dominant club. The Outlaws MC is a dominant club. The relationship is respected. That's it. Nothing more. Nothing less. Before I left, after eating, we shook hands once again briefly, nothing major, and I went my way with my daughter in arm. It was time to get this mission rocking. I went home to get ready.

I heard the truck engine outside rumble in idle. I immediately got up and threw on my hoodie. I knew what truck it was just from the sound. I dipped outside and came back inside moments later with the two rubber circles, one on each shoulder. The tires get tossed in the ol' lady's car, a phone call to the shop gets made, cash gets grabbed (always bring cash; I'll explain in a minute), rags get thrown on, garage door opener gets slapped, helmet strapped on, keys ignite, first gear shifted in, and we are off. I get tires installed, the price is dropped significantly because I pay off the books (hence the cash). The business saves on paying taxes, and I save with the price being dropped. That's a win/win. I don't do shit square if I don't have to. I've learned to search for the angles. The hood, the military, and this nation has taught me that. I get my tires installed, and I ride back home.

HOOD LODO

Time to load my gear and make moves. I take my throw-over saddlebags into the living room and start loading my piles in a methodical manner. The right saddlebag is my uniform and clothing items like black socks, black boxer briefs, black tees, black soft colors, black change of gloves, black masks, etc. The left saddlebag is my maintenance items and non-uniform related gear like my saddlebag shaped two-gallon extra fuel container, my trickle charger, a pouch of specially selected tools including relevant metric sockets and hex wrenches, the ratchet, my fully loaded flask. I put a bunch of other items in this bag because I packed so fucking tight I had some extra space, so I just kept packing shit. I put my personal hygiene kit in there, deodorant, and a bunch of other shit. Next is my tank bag in which I put road-related items like various eyewear and masks, a ten-ounce bottle I washed out and filled with forty dollars in quarters. I have no idea how many tolls I am going to run into, and my transponder was not going to arrive in time, so I just took a shitload of quarters. I took enough of my hypertension pills for two weeks. I put my multi-tool, Benchmade fixed-blade combat knife with 550 cord grip, a few pens, and shit like that in there.

All my gear is packed so there's nothing left to do but suit up. I promise you this is exactly how it happened: An unseen orchestra starts playing theme music personalized to me and the sound of violins and timpani fill the air. I pull the black boots on, stand up and strap that black belt firm, grab that black leather coat, a little tattered from having gone down in it a few times, and zip it up slowly. The zipper echoes harmonics off the walls. The light in the living-room dims automatically once I grab my duster. (The duster is our black oil-slicked trench coat designed for riding horses with protective strapping to go around your legs or cover your saddlebags. It's an iconic piece of the Outcast uniform. It serves other nefarious purposes as well, but it is one of our signature items now.)

I hold it out with a sharp shake in front of me. I let the fabric settle still before I swirl it from one side to the other and drape it over my shoulders. As the duster flies through the air, in slow motion, a choir of beautiful, naked, black women with black angel wings start softly singing an operatic note underneath the wind the duster makes cutting through the air. The duster drapes down and hangs off my shoulders. I grab my black leather gloves with the fingertips exposed and pull each one on. The sound of stretching leather makes the ears of the black cat in the windowsill raise. I grab the folded leather vest that lays ominously on the edge of the couch and open it. The sun, as it sets, glares off the words OUTCAST and a crack of thunder rips through the living room. The cat dashes from the window as the drapes and blinds float in the violent breeze that screams through the room. I place the vest on over the duster and button it from bottom to top pausing to ensure each button is firmly snapped. I pull it down sharply, grab my black leather kerchief and strap it around my neck. I palm my black helmet, and the choir of naked black women with black angel wings cry out! Their sound is joined by the wind! The Old Man on my back grins menacingly in the flickers of lightning that flash through the black clouds. A deafening crack of thunder explodes as the front door gets blown open, and the glasses in the kitchen rattle. I turn towards the ol' lady and say, "Well, I'll be going now." Her mouth is silent, but her eyes speak out, "Where you going, darling?" I gaze out of the doorway squinting my eyes and respond over my shoulder, "West." I walk out to that black horse, throw those black saddles on her, throw one leg over her, and mount her. I pull that black scarf up over my nose, pull those black goggles down over my eyes, strap that black helmet on with the spikes glistening in the last rays of sun. I turn that black key, and she awakens with her engine rumbling and her headlight peering down the path of our unwritten future. Together, that iron horse and I ride off with that duster in the wind. If one were to listen really closely, they could hear The Old Man on my back whisper to the choir of naked black women with black angel wings a simple word repeated three times: "Outcast... Outcast... Outcast..." (I mean, it might be possible that it didn't exactly happen like that, but we would be splitting hairs here).

Day One

  I make contact with Billy The Skin, in Detroit, and tell him I'm rolling out. I shoot a text out to Crash as well. I might be coming late as fuck, but I'm coming. The ride to Detroit is anticipated to take ten hours and it's mid-afternoon already so, yeah, I'm going to be coming in Night Wolf style. I'll take the time here to explain how I earned my Wolf Pack name. The rumor is I never slept. The Pack would be sleeping in our Wolf den, and a Wolf might get up to go take a leak, and there I was outside already. "Go to fucking sleep, dude, what the fuck!" I would come tip-toeing into the den an hour before we had a mission, from cruising the night, and maybe one of the wolves would be up early and say, "Where the fuck are you coming from?" There is a two-part answer to why I'm a night wolf: Afghanistan is so busy, and there is so much shit going on during the day that it seems like the war, and all the bullshit, just cools down for a few hours at night, and there is a serene calm to it. That calm I loved. It was my day-to-day sanity. I felt alive and had some seclusion in that calm. It would be just me and my dog, Scrapulous Maximus (Scrappy for short, which was some wild dog that I started training out there, and soon he just became my buddy).

  The other reason had to do with me being the QRF leader. We had several duties as Wolf Pack, and typically Alpha Wolf was in charge, but when we were QRF, which was a lot of the damn time, I was in command of the Pack. I monitored each military group that rolled out of the base on radios that I kept in my hut. While all the other wolves were sleeping, I was listening to all the different teams communicating with the headquarters element, reporting their checkpoints, and giving updates on their actions. I would listen to their internal communications on their respective freqs (frequencies) as well, so I had a mental picture of where everyone was and what they were doing in the battlefield. Even when I was sleeping I, kind of, still had a mental picture that was painting itself of the battlefield based on the information coming through those radios. I would have them on real low volume, but I would pay attention to them. This way if the Raven element, for example, started chattering on the radios that they see some suspicious activity, and they were going to check it out, I already knew exactly what route they were on. I knew how long it would take to get there, how many of them were out there, how many insurgents they suspected, what weapons they were carrying, etc. This way I could snap the Wolf Pack out of bed and have them fully dressed, guns fully loaded, Blue Forces fully tracking, and flying out of the gate in less than six minutes. It was because of the communication I had. Communication is everything. Otherwise, I would have to wait for Raven to report to Headquarters that they were in some shit, then wait for HQ to compile all the details and get an understanding of what it was and what to do. Wait for HQ to contact me, which they might do by sending a runner who might go to Alpha Wolf first, who then goes to me and tells me the details, and then I put the plan together and roll out. Fuck that inefficiency. That's how people get killed. That could take anywhere from twenty to forty minutes, especially if the Pack is all spread out. The minute I sense shit going south for an element we are supporting, from the information I'm monitoring, I start gathering the pack together. They are ready to snack on prey when the word comes down because of my nighttime vigilance. That nighttime vigilance earned me the name Night Wolf. (It also earned me a visit from the docs saying I was "hypervigilant". Yeah, I got you doc, but we are QRF, and vigilance is kind of what makes this work.) Don't get it fucked up, there would be times Sneaky Wolf or Crazy Wolf might come into my hut and damn near demand I went to sleep. I would pass one of them all the radios and they would monitor them, and I would get some shut-eye. My Pack took care of me. We all looked out for each other.

I hit the road. I have not even gotten on the highway yet, and I'm getting the looks. You just have to accept that shit when you are completely blacked out, have a full state rocker on the bottom of your cut, and a spiked mohawk on your helmet. Middle fingers up, let's ride. My GPS is working perfectly. I mounted it earlier with the new power source I hooked directly to the battery with a SAE connector. I hit Billy, who is now my POC (Point of Contact), in Detroit. I hit Three, who is my contact in the forward element, and I hit Grass who is my rear detachment. All the communication is out, so I'm good. I'm riding hard. The bike feels fucking great. She was making a squeaky, vibrating noise from the fuel tank when I took her out for breakout. I re-installed the fuel tank when I wired the USB port into the bike, and I added some homemade grommets so the squeaking had stopped. My bike sounds good. She is very quiet compared to everyone else's with their straight pipes and baffle-less bullshit, but I kind of like her silent. I don't like a loud bike (at the time). She has a deep rumble just to let you know she is on and rocking. Nothing more. Nothing less.

Anyway, I'm cruising for a while and burning through the state of Massachusetts. As powerful and sexy as our pack formations are, I'm enjoying the freedom of riding solo this time. It's faster than the pack. I command the road. I'm tearing down the highway very focused. I'm riding hard in the left lane when some dude in the far-right lane pulls up parallel to me, with one of his thumbs up and a questioning look on his face. This dude, who looks like some preppy tourist at some national wildlife park, points rapidly with his finger down at the pavement then gives me a thumbs up again. It's as if he's asking me a question. I'm

29

just staring at the dude. I have no idea what this groupie is trying to communicate to me. Now, I want you to imagine what he is seeing looking back at him. It's not like he can see my eyes, because I have reflective goggles on, so he is getting this blank face looking back at him. I also have my mask on which is the nose and mouth of a skull making it look like an actual skull is riding a motorcycle with an open mouth. So, some opened-mouthed skeleton is blank-staring back at him as he flashes finger signs at the skeleton. The dude throws his thumb up as a confirmation that I got what he was saying, which I didn't, and he falls back in his little economy car.

I don't like male groupies. I don't care what the context is. Unless you're six years old, and you want to be like me when you grow up, I don't like any dude acting like a fucking groupie. After *that* male groupie falls back in the slowpoke lane some *other* male groupie comes dashing up in front of me from the middle lane. He swerves in front of me in the fast lane, powers his window down, throws his arm out the window and repeatedly points sharply at the ground. Ok, what the fuck is going on? This is the second person throwing me a sign like this. I look down. I don't see any threats in the road? I really don't understand what the fuck is going on and why... Then I see something... Oh shit!... As I scan my surroundings to try and figure out what all the symbolism and hand gestures are about, the corner of my eye catches an object to my left. I whip my head down and glare toward my rear tire and, sure as shit, I see my entire left saddlebag dragging violently against the pavement. Not only is it dragging solidly against the pavement and shredding to pieces, but it is leaving a liquid trail, almost as if it's bleeding out on the highway behind us. I throw my directional on and cut across to the breakdown lane to see what the fuck is going on.

You've got to be shitting me! My saddlebag has snapped off its retainers and is dragging by the support strings I tied to the bike. It has been grated open and has released all the contents out of it. The reserve fuel canister has been dragging so much that it scraped a hole in it and spilled damn near all the fuel out. My trickle charger worked its way out and was dragging behind the whole situation while hanging on by its cord. I'm surprised it was still there. How the flying fuck did the bag come off? I hop off the bike and shut her down. These were brand new beautiful saddlebags! They got a lot of praise from my bros at breakout for their design with the external pockets, and how they were lockable and all. They are removable, throw-over bags. The manufacturer strongly suggested having a mount system, but I had throw-overs before and have been fine without a mount because how my bike's ass end is. They were never impeded by the shocks or anything. Well, these throw-overs attached with four metal twist connect locks on the inside of the bag. Well, every one of those twist connects ripped right the fuck off. So, this fucking bag was completely unsalvageable. What the hell am I supposed to do now? I started thinking outside the box. I'm looking at various straps and trying to analyze if I have any way of securing the bag to the bike and pushing forward. Got it! I always carry 550 cord and this is why. Any soldier worth their salt has 550 cord somewhere. We rarely end up needing to use it but, when we do, it's a life saver. 550 cord is several strains of twisted string inside nylon wrapping that has the tensile strength of 550 lbs (I can't say I would attempt to secure anything that weighs 550 lbs with it, but theoretically this is possible). I go to grab my 550 cord and... fuck! Yeah, the 550 was in the left saddlebag. My packing list that let me know all the last-minute shit I packed was also in the left saddlebag. I sat there for a while processing the whole scenario finally realizing there is no way to re-attach these bags. I have to sacrifice the bag. Not only do I have to sacrifice the bag but without one bag acting as a counterweight, over time, the second bag would shift right out from under the seat and I would lose that bag too.

HOOD LODO

I had to think of a plan. I emptied the last of the fuel that was still in the reserve container into my tank and tossed that to the side of the road. I grabbed the right-side saddlebag, sat on my bike, threw the bag on the tank and began to tie the support strings to the handlebars. I was going to continue to ride with the right saddlebag resting on my lap. I could not risk jury-rigging the thing to the back of the bike and losing all that gear too. It would have been better if I lost the right-side bag, which was uniforms and shit. I could always just hand wash what I had on if need be. However, the left-side shit was the important gear. I don't even know all that was in there. Fuck it. I gotta ride on. I will regroup when I get to Detroit. I cannot shake the sensation that I am behind on time. I push on, with the saddlebag on top of my tank bag, resting in between my legs. I lean forward to kind of wedge it all in and continue to ride out, Detroit bound.

Approaching tolls is a bitch. Tolls, period, are a bitch. The whole idea of tolls, in fact, is some bitch-ass shit. I just don't dig tolls at all. I, for some reason, thought that I would run into those tolls that had no attendants but a receptacle that said "Exact Change" on it. I imagined rolling by and throwing a fistful of coins then rolling on. I did not see one of those. I don't even know if they make those anymore. I know I have seen them in my life; I just can't remember where or when. So, I have a bottle full of quarters, but I find myself using dollars to pay these tolls anyway. Toll after fucking toll, same routine: Ride up, slap the saddlebag to the side so it hangs next to the handlebars, grab ticket, stuff it in tank bag, pull saddlebag up, ride to the next toll plaza, slap saddlebag to the side so it hangs, pull ticket out of tank bag, pay the bullshit, pull saddlebag up, and ride on. Same shit, over and over again. The sun has faded away. I'm unsure how many hours I have been riding. I was not counting my tanks, and I was not counting my miles. I was just riding. I don't exactly know why, but

32

the tollbooths were excessively bothering me. There are a lot of tolls on the East Coast and they are not cheap. If the whole trip is like this, it is going to be a pretty hefty fucking price tag. Whatever, I keep pushing forward.

Nighttime is on me, and I'm glad I have my New Jersey hoodie on. I'm telling you this fucking hoodie is just the perfect fit and the perfect material. The hood is not all pointy and silly looking like a fucking Ku Klux Klan hood. It's not oddly dimensioned like some of the cheaper quality hoodies out there. It's just a solid hoodie. I wear it with the hood up then put my skid lid over it and I'm good to go. It gets cold at night on a bike, and all those layers that look like you're overdoing it are needed. I change my gloves to my gauntlets to cut the cold wind from going up my sleeves while I'm at a gas station. I fill up and keep pushing, tank after tank, toll after toll. I've been riding for quite a while. Detroit is only four hours out or so, maybe less. It's deep into the night hours. There is a quietness in the air. It's a strange kind of sensation. I have been riding solo on the road for a while. I can't remember at this point when I had seen a car last. It seems like forever. I see a tollbooth ahead. I rumble slowly towards it.

It's odd how each tollbooth has its own decor to it. They pretty much look the same, but as you hit one after the other, you start to notice differences in shape and differences in their booths. Subtle differences but differences nonetheless. This approaching tollbooth was more overtly different. This tollbooth had all the fixings. It looked very *professional* (if a tollbooth could look that way). It looked important, which meant, to me, I'm going to pay an arm and a leg for this fucking stretch of road. I don't even know what state I'm in. I've been pushing forward and have been in the zone, thinking. Not deep thought but just kind of embracing the fact that I am actually riding across the entire nation. I'm allowing the fact that I'm already short on gear to sink in, but for some reason this seems to be a pattern. It always pans out this way for me. Whenever I have a challenge, it always has an asterisk that's special for me that adds that extra bullshit to spice it up. Like I need extra challenge in my life, because normal challenge is just not good enough or something. I'm rolling up to the booth ready to pull my toll ticket from the machine. There is a man at this booth? The pattern is typically a machine that spits out a ticket at one toll, then a human being you pay at the next and repeat, but there is a man here to give me a ticket instead of a machine I guess. My eyes read a placard that is on the wall of his booth, and it took me a second to register what the words meant. I mean, I fully understood them. Like, I can read and have pretty good comprehension skills, but situationally it just had not penetrated yet how much impact that silly little sign had. I mouthed the words to myself one more time just to, kind of, let it sink the fuck in what I was reading: "Welcome to Canada."

"...Welcome to... Man, what the fuck?" I couldn't help but lay that colorful language on my professionally dressed little border buddy. "What the fuck is this? This is fucking Canada? Like, for real?" He assured me that this was indeed the country that borders us to the north. He followed up with the standard question a professional border person like him would ask an individual attempting to cross into another country: "Do you have your passport?" I responded exactly as a surprised biker who had no intentions of traveling to another country might to this question. With a chuckle I say, "No, I don't have my fucking passport. Look bro, I'm trying to go to Detroit, and my GPS took me here. I don't know what's going on." He calmly exits his little booth and assures me this happens at least once a day. He explains that my GPS took me this way because, ultimately, it is a shorter route to cut through Canada in order to get to Michigan. He says it shaves two hours off of my commute. He is telling me all this as he paces to the rear of my motorcycle. I'm internalizing what he just said, and the idea that now the four hours left to

Detroit has just jumped to six hours is heartbreaking. I already had bros waiting for me. Now my arrival time is going to be close to 6:00 AM. The booth dude says, "What's your license plate number?" Fuck if I know. I'm like, "I don't know. It's back there. Uh, N-1..., something, something. I don't know." He says, "You got a plate?" I whip my head around to get a look at this dude, like what the fuck is wrong with him? How the fuck can you not see that, bro? His eyes are locked on the ass of my bike exactly where the plate is, so...? I hop off the bike, duster swinging behind me, and peer down at what he is looking at. It all makes sense now. Yup, I am looking at two license plate bolts, with two metal corners of a license plate surrounding the bolts still on the bike, but no plate. "The... wow... The uh, plate tore off," I say. "Whoa! They just tore off? This is not vandalism or anything?" he asks. I say no. "How fast were you going?" he asks in an amused voice. I'm not really that amused. He is still rather calm, and we get my plate number from my registration.

My hope that he was going to immediately tell me to loop around and head back to such-and-such route into United States faded as he told me to pull my bike up to a lot and that some officers would come and talk to me. I let out a sigh. I have no idea how this is going to go. I hear if you have a criminal record you will be fucked at the border. I have heard a whole bunch of shit. I did what he said. Two military looking officers in their mid-twenties come approach me and the bike. The youngest one, in his best assertive voice, commands me to shut off the bike, which I was doing anyway. He, kind of, confusingly and hesitantly tells me to get off the bike and to put my hands on the back of a police cruiser that was parked near us. He sounds unsure of himself, as if he is trying to remember the right procedures for this situation. He is not aggressive sounding or anything. He is trying, rather, to sound professional. I'm way too familiar with all of this through my military training and some experiences overseas. I've

35

done many detainee-ops. His partner, who appears slightly older than him, I can sense is a bit more in tune with the rougher sides of life and seems a little less pressured than this kid. The kid asks me to remove all the items from my pockets. I do. Well, I remove most of them. He starts to frisk me and feels something in my legs. I have leather riding pants on and then cargo pants under those leather pants, so I didn't remove some silly shit out of my cargo pants. He continued the frisk. His partner asks for my ID. I give him both my state license and my military ID. He confirms, "You're military?" No, fuck-face, I won that at Six Flags. "Yeah, I am," I say. He takes the IDs, walks inside the security office, and gives them to someone, then comes back out. The slightly timid one continues, "Do you have any hidden compartments in the bike, uh, under the seat or, uh anything?" Well shit, now that you ask, yeah, I got a stash spot with a quarter brick of uncut cocaine right there under the seat. I got about a thousand or so Mollys under the fuel tank. Oh shit, I almost forgot, I got some ricin in my exhaust pipe. I mean, since you are asking me so politely and shit, "Nah, you can take a look." I pull out my Gerber multi-tool (since I lost my 10mm wrench in the saddlebag) and remove the rear bolt holding my seat down. I'm under my seat so much it's the only bolt I keep in. I remove the seat and offer the border patrol dude a look. He is more concerned with trying to think what the next thing to do is than actually taking a look to see what's under my seat. He asks if I can open my bags to see if I have any weapons. I tell the dude I have a knife in my tank bag. Now, the dude earlier at the booth had asked me if I had weapons on me, and I said no, but I didn't expect to get frisked then. In Massachusetts, having a fixed blade knife of this length is a concealed deadly weapon charge right there. No ifs, ands, or buts. Here, the officer says, "Can you open it for me please?" I pull it out of the sheath. Now, even though the blade is pulled out of the sheath and fully exposed to the officer, he continues his memorized spiel

36

and asks the following question, "It does not have any mechanical opening, right?" I don't feel that question deserves a response, so I remain silent. "Ok, you should have no problem with that."

His partner speaks now. His tone is cool, "What's Outcast?" he asks. I say, "A motorcycle organization." He nods and continues, "What uh, is this club about?" "I don't understand your question?" I say. He rewords his question: "What made you select Outcast over another organization to try for? Are you all veterans or something?" I replied, "They ride hard. I wanted to ride with the best." The dude seemed more like he was thinking about joining Outcast as opposed to trying to probe me for information. He slid in a continuation of his last question, "Did you have to try out, or anything, for the club?" Oh, if he only knew! However, I continue pacifying the situation, "No, nah, you just gotta love to ride." I nod, to confirm the bullshit in my answer. He accepts it. Phbbt! If this guy could speak to one of our probies and ask them if they had to "try out". If this guy only knew our crossover process. If he could hear the cries or see the tears. If he could witness the pain or see the bruises. If he could understand the wisdom learned during this time. But, that is only for Outcast to know. His boy pipes back up, "Well, sir, you seem like an alright guy, you know. You're military and all. So, yeah, sir, you can continue through Canada if you wish, or you can go back through United States." What? Ha! Really? I don't know why I decided to make it seem like it was actually a choice I was making but I did, "Well uh, what is the benefit of either?" The partner advises me that two hours will be saved out of my trip if I go through Canada. Well, looks like I'm traveling through Canada, boys! They bid me farewell and I roll off. Wow! Fuck it.

I pull over right before getting on their highway to make contact with Billy and Grass. Billy tells me to be safe and that he has people waiting for me, just get there when I can. Grass reminds me to get my mother patch and asks me if I want him to call the mother chapter and make sure it's there for me. I told him to do what he thinks is necessary and that I would push on. I can tell by how Grass is responding that he is sparked up by my trek. I can almost see his sarcastic grin with his eyebrows up, waving a cup of Crown Royal on the rocks in the air, saying (with those exaggerated pauses in between his words when he drinks) "How... the hell.... you end up in Canada, bro?" and bursting into laughter before I even answer. I'm going to hear it when I get back. I push forward. This fucking journey is starting to feel like an obstacle course instead of a road trip. No worries though.

It is very early in the morning. The time is around 3:00 AM. I am cruising through the desolate streets of Canada. The country is completely foreign to me. It's so quiet. I don't understand the street signs. I am unfamiliar with the shapes of their signs. I don't even fully know what symbol they are using for gas out here. I have no understanding of the geography of Canada. I don't know if Montreal is over here, and Quebec is over there. I don't know if I'm in Ontario or anything. I think it was the first time during this trip I genuinely felt a sensation of vulnerability. It's crazy because I can almost promise you half of the occupants of Canada know where California and New York are and can probably tell you what road to go from Detroit to both. Last time I was in Canada I was eight years old. I have family somewhere in this place that I obviously don't keep in contact with. I keep looking at my GPS because, truthfully, I just want to get out of Canada. Nothing personal against Canada; it's just that being in another country when I'm not prepared for it is a pretty fucked-up feeling. I mean, think about it, I don't even know what the laws are. I don't have a fucking license plate and have no idea what happens if I get pulled over by Canadian police.

In the middle of this myriad of thought comes the perfect icing to this cake: My GPS on my phone looks me right in my fucking face and the screen says, "Where the flying fuck are you, bro, because I have no fucking clue." You gotta be fucking shitting me! GPS SIGNAL UNAVAILABLE. Now, really... now? Motherfucker! You've got to understand that I have been pushing through Canada for about an hour or so. It would be a fucking waste of life to try and push backwards to the border. I don't even think I could because I took a bunch of turns, here and there, and I could not backtrack that shit again on my best day. If I got lost, I would not even be able to tell by the city I was in that I was off track because I have absolutely no context of Canada. To add to this tragic comedy, at this exact moment, my low fuel light turns on. I have no idea how I'm going to find a fucking gas station. I decide to do the only thing I can, which is to rely on my instincts. I zone out and let the wind carry me in the direction I need to go. It's like being super alert and super passive to influence at the same time. I let my instincts carry me on, and it seems like it is working. I end up in some residential type of suburb of some sort and can see the neon glow of what looks like a gas station down the way. I ride towards it. It definitely is a gas station. I roll up to one of the pumps, and I try my debit card to fuel up. The pump tells me to go fuck myself. So I go inside to the Canadian who looks like a Mexican to pay for the gas and ask for directions. The Canadian-Mexican commences to tell me directions for about fifteen minutes. I have him repeat the directions. I repeat them, and I am guaranteed to get lost. He is unsure of certain parts of his own directions that have steps like, "Turn left when you see part of the mountain sticking out." This is not good.

I fuel up and respond to Billy the Skin's inquiry of where I am. I tell him my situation. He warns me not to wear my rags in Canada and explains, "They don't like us out there at all." I don't know about all that. I had a pretty pleasant time with my two border buddies out here, but whatever. I'm not hearing taking my rags off. First off, where the fuck am I going to put them? Secondly, what for? I am about to ride out, but I think about it for a second. This is a bro who is from the mother chapter telling me information about a country I have never been through. Maybe, just maybe, I should humble myself and take his advice. I'm pretty sure there is going to be a backstory involving Outcast fucking up Canada back in the day, or something that I am going to learn later. I go back and forth with the idea for a minute, then make my choice. With all the bullshit going on right now all I need is to get fucked over while in another country because of the rags on my back. I remove my Outcast vest, and I swear I heard what sounded like one of those black angels with the black wings cry out in pain. I don't know. Anyway, I push out following the mental directions that the Canadian-Mexican gave me.

There's no way this is going to work. I have been riding for way too much time without getting confirmation that I am going the right way. The way this trip is going I don't feel confident with this at all. I have to think wisely and enact some urban survival skills. Ok, bang, I got it. I pull over at a hotel that I see on a pretty well-lit strip. I walk into the concierge desk, duster floating behind me, and speak to the gay dude (I don't mean that disrespectfully, that's just how I remember him. He was flamboyantly gay). I pull my phone out to get the address, and I have the concierge print out Google-searched directions to the mother chapter in Detroit for me. He disappears into the back room and returns with the printout. I thank him and leave. Alright, I'm on my way to my iron. I take a gander at the sheet while walking through the parking lot; The shit is in French, and the distances are in meters. Whatever, I will make it work. I slip the directions into my tank bag's clear plastic map section, put my phone and inactive GPS away, pop the mini flashlight that I had in my tank bag in my mouth, and take off. So, I have a fucking saddlebag on my lap, a tank bag that is barely visible underneath the saddlebag, with Google directions in another language in it, that I am viewing with a flashlight that is hanging out of my mouth. *This* is how I ride out and continue my trek all the way to the border.

I ride through the quiet night stopping only to fuel up. I pay with American money but receive Canadian money as change. For some reason that bothered me more than it should. I was getting slightly fatigued, and it was making me aggravated as well. As the sun starts coming back up, I see the border to the United States. They allow me *into Canada* with no passport and no license plate on a bike from which I pull a fixed blade military combat knife, wearing a duster, a skull mask, and an outlaw motorcycle club vest, but coming back into the United States is another story. Yup, I get detained. It's not even worth expressing all the shit involved with this, 'cause it was not anything serious. I was just put in a room with a bunch of other people, told to follow a lot of rules while I waited for them to finally tell me I can push on, which they did after what felt like forever. It was just more time wasted. I rode on towards Detroit. My GPS was active again. I navigate and come into the city of Detroit, which you know you are in before you read any sign that tells you. There is the familiar, depressing décor of poverty that lingers in all hoods. It doesn't really matter what hood you are in. They all are very different with shit you only know if you live there but they are all the same as well. Poverty has no jurisdiction, wears no colors, and has no limit. It's everywhere, and it has the same characteristics. Anyway, I pull up to that signature "Mother Chapter Established in 1969" sign, swirl into the parking lot of the Detroit clubhouse, and see my brother named Asshole Kurly holding the clubhouse door open for me. I do a loop around the parking lot then ride my iron right through the door into the clubhouse. (Flashback: X-Ray, this is Night Wolf.

41

HOOD LODO

Checkpoint One reached, one vic, one pack, time 0725 hrs
how copy? over) Finally, I made it to Detroit.

Day Two

If anyone has seen Bizzy Bone, from Bone Thugz-N-Harmony lately, this is exactly who Asshole Kurly reminds me of. He got that long-ass west coast hair, the mannerisms of an east coast G, and talks like a southern pimp. My bro has been waiting on me since the night before. He looked as tired as I did. He slaps me a handshake with a mother chapter patch in his hand. Everything in Outcast is earned. You gotta hit the mother every year, but to get your patch it has to be on iron. I have been to the mother before, but now I earned my patch. Since I made it back into the States from Canada, I have been waiting to get to the clubhouse so I can crack open my flask, take a long swig, and catch a catnap. So, that's exactly what I went to do. Kurly and I were speaking lightly. He was more giving me my space and letting me settle in. I was talking about how fucked up shit has been to get here. I open my saddlebag and realize my flask was in the other saddlebag. It was filled to the brim with 120-proof Jamaican Rum and would have been a nice taste right about now, but nope. So I ask Kurly for a drink, and he says he doesn't have the keys to the refrigerators that contain all the alcohol. I look up and see them locked. He immediately gets on the phone to call for someone to come and unlock the alcohol, but I stop him. "It's all good bro, no worries." He asks me if I'm sure, 'cause he can have someone open up right now. I say, "I'm good money. I'm gonna catch some z's." I wasn't really in that mode. When I get to Cali and am with my bros, then I will probably go nuts, but until I get there I'm just focused on making sure I get there.

I dip to the back room where the couches and shit are and crash. I can't really sleep though. I know that resting, even if it is not full REM sleep, is still beneficial for the type of riding I'm doing. So I do just that. I rest for about three hours before I hear Kurly talking about me to an old school sounding bro. He's right to the point with all his questions. He sounds like he just showed up for work and is finding out what his assignment is. Apparently, it's me. He walks over to the back room, and I'm already on my feet in the darkness waiting to meet him. He introduces himself as Kulumbo. I introduce myself, "Hood. Massachusetts." He asks me if I'm ok. I say, "Yeah, I'm good, just resting." He asks me if I ate and suggests I have some breakfast. He names different types of locations then suggests I just ride with him. I do.

His hospitality is different. It's unique in its presentation. It's not the celebratory, festive, rah-rah-rah outlaw type of show. Kulumbo has been around. His servitude is an example of the durable type of Outcast hospitality that is a non-negotiable duty as a bro. It's what you do. You take care of your bros, period. That is what he was gladly doing. He took me to get some food. Fried fish with hot sauce and fries, which seems to always be a dish that ends up in front of me whenever I have on an Outcast vest in another state. I reach into my pants pocket and pull out my wallet, and Kulumbo, almost disappointedly, says, "No, no, no man." He pays for my food.

He is ready to get to the next order of business, which is what I'm going to do about my saddlebag situation. We brainstorm for a bit on who can install some bags for me. Again, in the spirit of taking care of his bro, Kulumbo is prepared to take me to whoever, for whatever, in order to get new saddlebags. I already had an alternate plan of just transposing my saddlebag content into a backpack and rolling out that way until I get back and can reassess the best approach for carriage. He takes me to a military surplus store, and we go shopping for a suitable backpack. I swear, everything in a military surplus is over-priced, outdated stuff for wannabe military nuts and collectors. Don't get me wrong, you can find good shit in there; Just 'cause it's used by the Army though does not make it five times better, but you damned sure will pay five times the price. I know all this gear, because I got issued this stuff. I end up leaving there with an all-black Alice Pack. The same Alice Pack I was issued when I first joined the military in the year 2000. Ironically, I joined the military in Charlie Company 1/46th Infantry, and our company name was "Wolfpack". I began as a Wolfpack. Almost two decades later I wear a Wolf Pack badge under my collar as a wolf in a completely different Wolf Pack. It was destined.

The familiarity of putting that rucksack on again was strange. It's like visiting a house you used to live in as a kid. They don't issue these packs anymore – we have advanced to MOLLE (Modular Lightweight Load-carrying Equipment), which is used by several NATO forces – but, it will do for this trip just fine. I purchase the pack, and we walk to the car.

Before I even get in he tells me he got a dude inside the motorcycle store that can sew my patch on. I feel good about that. I just expected to go home with my patches and square all that shit up there. I get my patch sewn on, and Kulumbo, who doesn't even wear his Outcast vest, scoffs at bikers who wear all these masks but their face is on their license. He has a calmness to him but a slight bitterness as well. Maybe, "bitterness" isn't the word, but he has a hue of disappointment in the results of the current motorcycle community, and it taints his speech.

We roll out, and he gives me a tour of Detroit. Again, it's not some festive, "let me show you all the sexy shit in my city" type of tour. Nah, it's more like the result of what happens when you are in a car with someone who has been in a city long enough to have a story for every block. The only tourist-feeling shit we went to was the Motown Museum. "Take some pictures for the ol' lady," he says. I hop out and assault the building. I breach the perimeter, snap a few pics, and exfiltrate back to the car in, like, thirty seconds. I'm not a touristy picture-taking type of dude.

We ride some more, speaking heavily about Outcast from Kulumbo's perspective. He becomes increasingly expres-sive as I probe him for his opinions. He draws a contrast of what it used to be, what it is now, and why. He speaks of the good, the bad, and what just *is*. I listen. We pass a significant building in the Outcast Nation's history. He tells me this is so-and-so's place (I leave the name out because who I am speaking about only matters to Outcast). He allows me to do some recon while he gives me the intel he has on how that division has manifested itself. That's all I will speak on that. The mother chapter and all its members carry a lot of weather with them. It is the weight of experiences that range from great times to impossible times and everything in between. You can see and feel it.

We arrive back at the clubhouse, and other bros are starting to show up as well. Dino comes through, pauses, looks at me, cracks a smile, and walks behind the bar. He opens the fridge. "You want something to drink, man?" I'm shoveling pieces of fish into my mouth. "Yeah, a beer. I don't care what it is." I dig in my pockets as he grabs a Corona. I remember from the last time I was in the mother chapter that the prices are cheaper than my clubhouse. "Put that away," he commands in disgust. "You a guest, bro." Fair enough to me. My drinks are on the house. Other bros such as Long Time and Hunnit start chilling and talking with Asshole Kurly and myself. A girl from a support club is in the clubhouse expressing how she wants to be an Outcast PO but she is loyal to her club and her dude and bla bla bla. The dude she is referring to is a fifty-something year old white guy, and she has got to be, at most, twenty-three years old. So, of course, I believe everything she is saying about loyalty to her dude and all that fly shit. Not

46

that I am saying it is impossible that she is. However, her mode of movement does not feel like it matches up with her words. I just want to remind y'all that I am hearing this while we are inside an Outcast clubhouse, and ol' girl has Kurly in one ear, the rest of us on the other side of her, and it's midafternoon.

We are all just shooting the shit. I'm listening to bros talk about who got shot and other hood stories. Some chick shot up some people outside someplace a few days ago. Then she got killed. "You want some of this fish, bruh?" I offer. Bros are good. I help Long Time clean the floors. I ask him how he got his name. He explains that bros would say he wasn't going to get his rags for a *long time*. He says he was hard-headed and stubborn as a probie. His demeanor seems like someone who is genuinely humbled at this point. The silver lining on that cloud, I guess, is that the fucking floor was swept and mopped in, like, minutes. Being that he has been doing it for a long time, that motherfucker got that shit down to a science!

I see a figure and hear a voice coming through the doorway. The sun is beaming so it's just a silhouette. The silhouette gets deeper into the room. I start making out the face as his eyes start to adjust from the sun. We both recognize each other at the same time. "Ohhhh shit! Ahhh!" he says, and before I know it Tee has me in a bear hug and is swinging me through the air. "I heard a bro came through from Massachusetts. I didn't think it was you! Oh shit! This one of my favorite bros right here!" The sentiment is shared. Not because we have been through some wild shit together yet. There are bros you just click with instantly, and that's just what it is. We clicked like that. Tee is one of those bros who lights up the place because he is always beaming. I remember the first time we met, and the conversation somehow went into discussion about the book, *The Art of War*. That was it. Tee gave me a look after that conversation, and he took a liking to me. It wasn't anything dramatic; it just is some people

47

rub you the wrong way until you get to know them, and some you just vibe with. Tee and I vibed well from the first time we met back in Savannah. We've been good ever since.

The Detroit bros are preparing for a party that's going down in the clubhouse later in the night. I'm starting to plot my next destination. The bros are assisting me by making contact with bros in other clubhouses, pulling maps out, and we are all discussing the next house I should hit. Although Tee is on the phone with bros in Kansas City setting up my next move, the other bros are speaking as if I am going to leave tomorrow. They are laughing like, "Bro, you gonna chill a little more, then the party kicks off, and you know you ain't gonna wanna leave then." As likely as that may be, it's not what is going to happen. I more than appreciate the hospitality at the mother chapter but I'm on a mission, and I have to keep pushing.

I pack my gear into my rucksack. This pattern is so familiar, it is alarming me. The two worlds of military and Outcast have been parallels, but now they are starting to smear into each other a little bit. When I was home, I was loading Outcast gear, and then I was loading military gear. Now, I am loading Outcast gear *into* military gear. My brain is getting triggered in strange ways. I'm unlocking that soldier mode but in an Outcast setting, and I can feel it happening. I strap the rucksack on my back and exhale as I embrace the feeling of that familiar weight in those familiar places. I instinctively pull the side straps, cinching it tight on my back. I walk outside. I have no duster trailing behind me this time. It's packed in the ruck.

The sun is out and it feels good. Tee is explaining to me why his bike looks like it just slid into home plate. The bike is fucked up. Lights are dangling, and it obviously recently got laid down. So he is running the story down to me: He tells me how he was riding somewhere, and how he was giving double middle fingers up while he was riding, like he does, but this time, when his hands went back to the bars he squeezed his front brake too firmly. We all know what happens after that. The front wheel locked up, and that's all she wrote. Tee is one of those dudes that could walk in with half a bike because the other half got ran over by a train and still have that excited, big-ass smile on his face. The dude has a radiance to him. He's a good bro.

I don't want to leave, but I have to. More bros are pulling up. I'm talking to one bro in the parking lot about his iron, which has car speaker cones that he drilled into the windshield. The windshield is not a stock windshield but a piece of plexiglass attached to the bike. It's as close to a rat bike that I have seen so far in the nation. I heard a bro make a comment, "That's good, though. Most bros say they are going to keep moving, but they never do. They party and shit, but you stuck to it." I didn't respond. Kansas City is my next destination. (X-Ray, this is Night Wolf. Permission to SP? Destination: Kansas City, one vic, one pack, time 1259 hrs how copy? over) I revved up, gave my final salute, and took off, Kansas City bound.

I left Detroit for, like, ten minutes and already was missing the place. There is a certain feel to the mother chapter that is unique. There really is. Not in a good way, not in a bad way. In a unique, dark, Detroit, Outcast MC way. I'm pounding towards Kansas City. My GPS says twelve hours. I'm pushing tank to tank. I can't shake the concern of falling too far behind so I'm moving with a purpose. As far as my calculations and how many days I have, I think I should be good. I feel like one with my motorcycle for real.

I have two bikes. I still ride the first one a lot. I push her pretty hard, but she can take it. I ride her, and I feel like I'm on top of her when I do, 'cause I am. My second one, the one I'm on for this trip, however, has a whole different feel. She is a beefier, more aggressive bike, but she sits lower than the first one, which makes her just as nimble as the lighter one. Her handlebars make me lean just a little bit more over her, but her footrests are lower, so it works out perfectly. We end up being a compact unit that solidly pushes through whatever situation. I feel like I am *in* her, as opposed to *on* her. When we ride it doesn't feel like I'm just cruising; it *feels* like I have somewhere to go. It's all in the posture. The same way being in command of your posture when you stand and when you walk can change your confidence (or can reflect your lack of), such is the way with your posture on a motorcycle. There is the aerodynamic lock-in that you might have on a street bike that is fully committed to aerodynamics, but how awkward of a posture that is waiting at a red light. There is the far opposite of that spectrum with the cruiser custom with the ridiculously high ape hangers that spreads you completely the fuck out. The exact opposite of aerodynamic. You are a big star of drag, sucking up wind, tearing through the highway. I get it. Well my bitch is neither. Or better yet, she is both. She is a cruiser, undoubtedly, and she sits so low that I can hunch back and am firmly planted with my legs spread at a red light like a cruiser, but she is an attack cycle as well. She is, at any moment, ready for you to lean forward and suck your knees into her tank and turn into a motherfucking torpedo. I would have it no other way. The bike matches my character, which is important, especially on a trip like this. You don't want to fight your bitch. You might be able to hide it bar hopping, but for a journey like this you can't hide the truth in your relationship. Either you and your motorcycle are a team or you're not. No one can give you advice on this relationship either, because when that truth comes out, whatever it is, you and only you have to deal with the consequences. Meditate on that.

Aww shit! Fucking rain! Out of nowhere it just starts pouring little painful pellets of water that I am slamming into and I'm not dressed for. I push forward into it, trying to see if it's worthwhile to pull over and modify my gear. The rain fights back and doubles in intensity. No worries. I pull over under a bridge for a wardrobe change and a quick piss break. The duster comes back out of the ruck. The mask changes from my stretchy cloth skull to my leather handkerchief. The gloves go from my open fingered leather to the gauntlets. Leather pants make their second appearance and go over the cargo pants. Ok, leg over bike, kick stand up, clutch in, gear down. "Fuck you, rain!" I scream out from under the bridge, and I hear The Old Man on my back give a hefty, ghostly chuckle that echoes in reverb against the bridge walls. Less than a tank later I can see the light blue sky down the road. It's the light at the end of the rainy tunnel.

Before I know it, I'm right back to slamming those miles down. I can't really say I'm tracking signs, towns, states, and all that jazz. I'm just pushing through trying to make sure I hit gas stations when I need to. I think I was in the corner of Ohio, or maybe the beginning of Indiana, at some little gas station, doing the same routine I have been doing: Pull over, helmet on right mirror, goggles on left, mask pulled down, step off bike, gloves on seat, pay for fuel, open the tank, fill up. I have been pulling over every hundred and ten or so miles. It allows me to track how many miles I have been doing when I can just count them in hundreds. I usually get 146-156 miles out of my tank, but this trip I have been getting less. Let me fill my tank completely to the top and start stretching these stops out. I usually just fill her up while she is leaned over, but this time I leg over the bike and straighten her up off her kickstand so I can get more in the tank. Ok, suit up time. I got pavement to pound. Where the fuck are my gloves. I'm sitting on them. I pull them from underneath me, slip them on and burn out of there and back on the highway.

I have never been to Kansas City before. I have been pounding for some hours, and the little rest I got in Detroit is starting to show its face. I'm fatigued a little bit.

51

HOOD LODO

Dusk is starting to settle in. It must be close to an hour and a half I have been riding since the last fuel stop, and I stretched this tank pretty far. I see a secluded gas station. I better hit this one. These stations are starting to get more and more spread out, and I don't have my reserve two-gallon saddlebag-shaped gas tank anymore, so I gotta be careful. I pull into the station, select my pump, and start my same gas station routine: Helmet off and on set the right mirror, goggles on the left, face mask pulled down, get off bike and pull gloves off, key in fuel tank, grab wallet, and pay for fuel.

That's one thing, with all these layers, you need to be mentally aware of and consistent with all that's in each pocket. My wallet I keep in the gun pocket of my leather coat. Maybe not this time, because it was not in there. If not there I might have put it in the gun pocket of my vest, then. I unsnap the button on the inside of my vest. Hmph, not there either. I check my pants pockets, nothing. What the fuck? I brainstorm real quick because other than those pockets I pretty much have been purposefully avoiding my other pockets, but I check all my pockets and my tank bag again just to make sure. I run through my vest gun pockets, my duster external pockets, internal pockets, my leather coat gun pockets, my leather coat external pockets. I slap the fronts of my leather pants and the back. I jimmy my hands into my cargo pants underneath my leather pants. I know I have it, so I just gotta remember where I put it when I was at my last fuel stop. I recall I put my helmet on the right, goggles on the left, and pulled my mask down. I got off the bike, put my gloves down on the seat, paid for the fuel, fueled up, then... Wow... Woooooow! I remember I sat back on the bike to straighten it up and put more fuel in it. I sat on everything I put on my seats. I remember pulling my gloves from under my ass before I rolled out. I had placed the wallet on the seat as well. Which means when I pulled my gloves from underneath me...Fuck. That empty feeling of defeat started to take over. That was over an hour and a half ago, and over a hundred and thirty miles in the other direction. The wallet must have fallen right in front of the pump in plain sight. There is no way in hell that motherfucker is still going to be there. The only hope is that someone turned it in, or if staff snatched it up. I know the four hundred or so in cash is a wrap, but if I could get the debit cards and my IDs, I'd be fine with that.

I pull the bike over to a parking spot and think what my next moves are going to be. I chuckle real quick because of how not-funny the situation is. First, I roll out by myself because of all the weird shit with my tires and bros, who said they were going, not going. I lose my gear in my saddlebags. I end up at border patrol and get flipped in Canada. I no longer have plates on my bike. My GPS cuts out, and I have to figure my way out of Canada. I figure my way out but get detained in the United States. Now this. It's like this trip is testing my tolerance, patience, endurance, and mental toughness. Deep down, this trip really excited me for so long, because I knew it was going to give me that feeling like I was on a mission again. I needed that, but this shit is pushing it with the unnecessary bullshit. I don't have any fucking cash. My bank cards are in that wallet. My bank card with my account numbers written on it is in there. Three military IDs are in that wallet, and trust me, mostly every soldier you know is only supposed to have one. I won't even get into that. My government credit card is in there. My expired license and my new license with two different addresses are as well. Like, the more the items come to me of what was in the wallet, the more daunting the whole shit is. You have everything you need to fuck my world up if you know how to do that shit. Fuck!

Ok, panicking is not my style; it never has been, so let me think of a plan quickly and start acting on it. My phone is powered from my bike and my bike has no fuel, so ultimately, I am on a limited power source with the phone. I will first call my bank and track down my last transaction, which should be that gas station. They can give me the address, then I can Google that, get the phone number, and at least ask them if they have the wallet. It's my only shot. I get my bank's phone number from Google and call. I go through all the bullshit to get a person on the line from card services. They want my account number. I don't fucking have my account number. I'm thinking, "Can't you ask me a bunch of verification questions to confirm it's me?" Nope. Fuck. Ok, I call the ol' lady and ask her to look in my checkbook and give me the account number, and I let her know what's going on. I call the bank back and go through the bullshit to get back on the line with a real person. They tell me they cannot see the address of the last location, but they tell me the zip code for which the transaction comes up. I take that information and try to figure out what route and state I was just in so I can narrow it down to what chain of gas stations it was. I go inside the gas station I'm currently at to get geographical info and routes from the teller.

Nighttime is starting to fall in. Worse comes to worst, I am going to have to wrap up in my duster and sleep on my bike. I can't get a motel, or any bullshit like that with no cash or IDs. I shoot a text out to Grasshopper just to let him know I'm fucked up in the game. I have been letting him know my progress here and there, so I shoot him and Three a text letting them know I'm fucked. I don't expect any response, but at least they know not to fucking expect a text from me saying I'm in Kansas City. Maybe they can make contact with KC or something at some point. Right now, I need to figure this out. I'm online on my phone trying to follow up on what the gas station was that I was at, but I keep getting interrupted by a flood of texts now. Grass is replying asking me where I am and can I backtrack and bla bla bla. The ol' lady is hitting me. I don't want to cancel the card yet just in case someone actually turned it into the teller at that gas station. I don't want to fuck myself in that sense. Fuck! Ok let me think.

Now Grass is calling. "Yo?" I say. He asks me some bla bla bla shit. I tell him what I got going on now and how I might have the ol' lady try and track down the gas station on the computer at home. Then I can use the phone and start canceling cards and what not. "Whoa, whoa, whoa! Listen bro…" he starts. "Call your ol' lady and tell her to relax. Don't start getting her all worried, bro." Grass continues and says one of the most significant phrases in this story. He says, "If you're in a club, and the club can't help you, then what's the point of being in a club?" Meditate on that. He shut me the fuck down right there. Like, instant humbling, because he had a point. In that sentence, I immediately realized how much I have not allowed Outcast to truly penetrate my world. Not because I didn't want to, but because I just did not know how.

The truth comes out in war, as in you flee to who you trust when you are in danger. You protect who you truly love when they are threatened. The truth comes out in challenge. I was being challenged, and I definitely did not think of tapping into Outcast for help. I never ask for help. I have come to believe if I can't do it for myself then it can't be done for me. For years, a lot of years, the only person besides my nuclear family that has gone above and beyond the call of duty to help me has been my wife. When I was at war all those times, she held it down. When I was locked up, she was there every visit. When I fucked up somewhere and was assed out, she would drop everything, silently, and arrive. Never spoke much about it; she just did it. Never complained about much, just expressed concern if she saw a bad pattern. When I got stabbed in the head, she changed those dressings. When I got drunk multiple times and pissed in the closet or next to the trash or on her box of shoes, she would scrub the urine. When I had something somewhere and needed it moved somewhere else in a hurry… Bang. I never got her involved, but she wouldn't ever give me those fucking speeches you don't want to hear. She never gave me that look you don't want to get.

HOOD LODO

She knew if I was doing it, it had to be done and was being done as safely as I could for the both of us. She trusted me. I trusted her. It showed. Well, Grass was asking me to trust Outcast. Let me reword that: the fucking universe was using Grass to relay a message and lesson to me. It got my attention. Not to remove anything from Grass at all, but the way this trip was going it was more than just Grass that was at work here.

Grass and I come up with a plan real quick. Much of it is me waiting for Grass to call me back with what the plan is. He calls Black Ice (my sponsor), this person, and that person, and bang and boom. My phone is going off here and there and before you know it, literally in minutes, the dust had settled, and I had a point of contact back in Kentucky named Big Tay. I still had the bottle of toll quarters, which was enough to fill my tank and get me there. Big Tay had an address to a hotel all set up for me. Step one was to get me to the hotel to regroup. Step two was to get money wired to me, of which Black Ice was in command. He was already on it. The shit was crazy to me! Like seriously, the shit was crazy! We don't fully know if this plan is going to work. We don't know if you can wire money without IDs and shit; we just don't know everything right now, but what we do know is that my journey is not stopping at this gas station. What I know is that somehow, once again, I am pushing forward. I also know now that this trip is more than just an attempt to make it across the nation on a motorcycle. It's more than making a mandatory national meeting for a motorcycle club. It's more than rekindling feelings preserved from wars I fought in the past. This is a unique mission of its own in a war I am fighting currently. It is a quest for which I will only fully receive the inherent wisdom when I get to California. It's my own yellow brick road, and I have not even made it to Kansas yet. I was invigorated, at least at that moment. Exhausted underneath, but I have to push on to the hotel in Kentucky where Big Tay is waiting for me. So, I fuel up

Toto, kickstand up, clutch in, gear down, and *vrooom*. On the yellow brick road I go with my headlight blazing making my way to Kentucky.

The location I have to go to in Kentucky is going to be more than a tank of gas, but I have just about what I would need in quarters. There is zero room for mistakes now. I push forward. I'm tired, but I'm in Night Wolf mode, which means underneath is genuine sleepiness. However, I am still able to function and perform for an extended period of time. When I do turn down I am going to crash, but that's after I get to my destination. I'm squinting while looking at my GPS and tearing through the highway. Big Tay is texting me, but I can't really check texts while my GPS is rocking. I will check it when I get to the next fuel stop. All that phone traffic and data usage has significantly drained my phone's battery and even though it's plugged into the power source it is taxed down to a very low percentage. With the GPS on, the power source seems to simply maintain the battery where it is, not really charge it. So each additional text and phone call and all that crap is slowly depleting the little juice that is left. I keep pushing and pushing. I'm fucking flying on my horse in attack posture with my duster flying behind me. I turn off an exit that says there is some fuel somewhere. I pull over on the side of the off ramp and check my messages.

Big Tay has changed hotels on me, and I have a new address now. I punch that address in the GPS. It's farther than where I originally was going. I continue off the ramp. My phone rings exactly at that moment. It's Big Tay. Impossible for me to answer the phone right now with gloves back on and all that shit. I'll call him at the gas station in a few minutes. What could he be calling me for? I couldn't help but think it had to be an additional challenge, but I think that was just the pessimism I now had from the pattern of this trip. I pulled into the gas station. Now I'm hypervigilant to all my actions and aware of all my gear at each fuel stop because of what happened in Ohio. I triple check each item I grab and put down. I need to get the bottle of coins to go and put some fuel in my tank, but let me call Big Tay first. I swipe and tap into my call log, see Big Tay's number, press the phone emblem to call him, and at that moment the screen turns into the swirling LG graphic and releases that chime of death right before it goes black. It then displays that annoying fucking message with the cartoon looking depleted battery, BATTERY NEEDS MORE POWER TO TURN ON. Motherfucker! Son of a bitch! See? I try to calm down and tell myself, "Nope, this is just part of the challenges ingrained in this quest. I will remain calm and think of the solution." That was the mantra I immediately created on the spot to exercise my patience.

I pulled my rucksack off, fished around in one of its compartments, and pulled out the wall charger for my phone. As I'm doing this, a man who pulled into the gas station after I did exits his pickup truck and starts walking toward me. I really don't have the fucking patience, yo. I'm tired. I'm fucking frustrated, I'm damn near pissed the fuck off, so the chances of this going pleasantly are pretty much next to none. I have no idea what fuckery is about to come out of this man's mouth. He pauses at a respectful distance from me and alerts me that my taillight is out. I look at my tail light and it's blacked out so I tap it. It flickers on then goes back out. Perfect. The dude says he rides too and he advises me to get that fixed, because that's how riders die. Yup, just add it to the list of bullshit. No plate, no license, no cash, no ID, and now no taillight. Police are inevitably in my future. It's already written. I thank him and walk into the gas station, count out a bunch of stacks of quarters, ask the clerk for fuel and an outlet. He points one out to me next to the counter. I plug my phone in, fuel up my bike, then pull up to a parking space to wait for my phone to get enough juice to power on.

I go in to check its progress, and who rolls into the gas station? You guessed it, the fucking fuzz. The police.

They slowly roll up and park right in the parking spot next to my bike. The ass of the bike is mooning the officer as he gets out of the cruiser. He damn near taps the missing plate with his door to get out of the cop car. I'm just watching the whole shit unfold. They both walk into the gas station, I'm fully ragged out and all that. I square up ready for the bullshit questions that are about to precede whatever they are about to do. "How's the ride tonight?" says, the cop as he passes me. "It's alright," I say, stunned by his nice guy shit. He purchases whatever cops purchase from gas stations and walks out of the door as I'm holding my phone. "You have a good night," he says. "Uh, yeah, you too." I know for a fact I was not concealing the screw face that resulted from that shit. I was in awe. This fucking trip is too much for me. A cop just being nice for no reason? If this was the East Coast... No way in hell.

I need to go to sleep for real. All these emotional woes are draining me. I power on the phone and call Tay from inside the gas station. He asks my location and says he has work in the morning. I tell him to take off. He says, "Nah" and that he is going to wait for me. He tells me to make sure I go to the last hotel he sent. I say, "Ok" and dead the conversation. I suit up and hit the road again. I'm fucking speeding because I'm tired, it's nighttime, and I just want to sleep. Those three hours in Detroit just are not cutting it. I have about forty miles or so left. I'm burning it up. I finally get to the hotel parking lot. I cannot wait to just go to whatever room and crash. I see I have messages I have not seen, and one of them is from Big Tay that was sent about the time I was pulling into the gas station earlier. It's a third hotel address, and that must be the last one he was talking about. I'm at the second one, which is the wrong hotel. It's like the straw that broke the camel's back. This fucking journey just keeps throwing straws on this fucking camel's back. It's damn right annoying, and I'm bullshit now. Luckily, the other hotel is only a few miles away. I speed the fuck off back on the journey. I just want to get to the fucking hotel and rest.

I'm there. I park right in front of the doors, gather all my shit and clunk towards the front desk. My helmet feels like it's a thousand pounds, and the rucksack feels like it's fused to my back. I say someone has a room for me and bla bla bla. She hands me the key. "Second floor on the right." I go to the room. There is no Big Tay. In a way, I'm relieved. I just want to crash. I walk in and take a look out of the window. Empty parking spaces outside of my window are beckoning for me to move my bike there instead of parked in front of the doors. I feel like around every corner is a catastrophe waiting to happen. The last thing I need is to wake up and my bike was stolen or something. I go back downstairs and move the bike to the parking space right under my window. I go back upstairs. Now I can sleep. I slide my key in the slot and nothing happens. One more straw? I slide the key again and nothing happens. Yup, another straw. I go back downstairs. A family is in the hallway and the lady says, "Cool outfit! Do you ride a motorcycle?" I let her husband, in his square-ball way, chew her out, "Well, honey, of course he does. Why else would he...." bla bla bla. His words lose my attention. I'm drained. I'm downstairs now. I get the receptionist to encode another keycard. She tells me to keep it away from my cell phone. I go back upstairs. It works. I'm in.

Sigh... Probably the best feeling of the whole trip was getting into that fucking hotel that night. Well, at least at that point it was. Big Tay had set up a late checkout and everything. I shot him a text letting him know I touched down and how much I appreciated the bro looking out. Shower, then sleep was the order of business. So that's exactly what I did. No idea when I was going to shower again, or *if* I was going to shower again so I just seized the opportunity.

Day Three

Sunlight starts to crack through the window of the hotel room. I could definitely just lay out for another four hours. I would be wasting time if I did so. There is too much to figure out and do. I feel different this morning. I'm well-rested and all, but I mean my attitude is different. I can't really put my finger on it, but it's militant and familiar. I immediately start plugging into my Outcast support structure. I hit Black Ice with the location of the money drop. I hit Big Tay to organize how to pay him for the location. The phone livens up with messages. Ice got the green light from Shooter to push the money forward. Big Tay tells me not to worry about it and that he just wanted to make sure I was good. I got his address, name, and all that fly shit, so I already know I'm going to take care of the bro, because that was some appreciated shit he did. Grasshopper calls on the phone, and we discuss phase two. He confirms that I am funded now by the club. He says I have options to push forward or to go home. Three Piece is confused and is texting me that I need to go home. He reasons that if I lost all my shit, and I am closer to home than I am to Cali, then I need to turn around. Three is not fully recognizing all the pieces that are in play right now. He does not know how many bros are aware of this mission. He has no idea that Mayday and Big June in Missouri are contacting me and waiting for my arrival. He has no clue that Tee, Kurly, Kulumbo, Billy, Long, and all of them in Detroit are tracking my movement and are waiting on the word that I made it to Kansas City. He does not know that Shooter co-signs me pushing forward, Grass is over-watching, Black Ice is doing the footwork, and Fullback is pushing forward to me the addresses to all the clubhouses across the nation. He is not aware of all this, but, more importantly, Three is not embracing an aspect of Hood that possibly he, and many others in the organization, have not gotten the opportunity to see, which is the fact that once that switch turns on, and I am in mission-mode, I don't stop. It took so much energy to get in this deep. It would take the same energy to pull out. It is a senseless way of approaching this challenge.

I put my phone down for a moment and really internalized the text message I just got from Three. I spoke the last part of the text out loud, "...You need to go home!" I thought about the meaning of those words. This is a mission now. It never was some fun, cross-country touring event. It was, and is, the fact that we have to be at a certain location by a certain time. That's all that matters. You either make it there, or you don't is how I was viewing this. If you make it, then you completed the mission. If you don't, then you failed. That's the end of it. No one cares or needs to care why or how reasonable it was that you didn't. The only relevant fact is that you failed, and your reliability meter just dropped a notch. Reliability is that one quality you never want to tarnish because it destroys trust, and when trust is gone, entire organizations crumble. You would want a reliable brother next to you, right? You would want a reliable soldier covering you, right? So the only question that each of us should be asking ourselves as we embark on missions and encounter challenges and mishaps is this: Can I continue? If the answer is "yes", then it's not a fucking question. That's what the fuck you do. Period. You do it for your team. You do it for your squad. You do it for your club. You do it for your family. You do it for your fucking self, so that when you look in the mirror in the morning you see a solid and reliable character looking back at you. You have pride in that person. You do not shy away from the eye contact that person is giving you, because in those eyes is the same pride being returned. You do it because it has to be done. You can always find a reason to quit. Justifiable reasons to quit are always there in every situation. It is your choice if you decide to tap that button. Fuck that button. Rip that bitch out of the console. "Can I continue?" That's the only question you need to ask yourself. If you have the mental capacity to formulate those words. If you have the breath to speak those words. If you have the time to ask that question, then the answer is already written. The answer is yes. So, keep fucking pushing. Way more is at stake than just not making it across the country. Having a failed mission in my personal, mental resume and tarnishing the sense of self-reliability I have built up is what is at stake. This is the delicate process to maintaining self confidence that I pay attention to and build in my soldiers, my daughter, and in people I care about. This is a little bit of how it's done. I wouldn't want any of my bros to move any differently.

I may be making this way bigger than it needs to be. Three Piece had more than valid reasons to suggest what he was suggesting. Under the circumstances, it would be very reasonable for anyone else to collapse back and take the trip for what it was worth. I'm not even the president or vice-president of my chapter, so, technically, it is not even mandatory that I be there. All of this is true, but there is another way of looking at this mission that is also true: Whenever life challenges you there are always justifiable reasons to stop pushing forward. There are always opportunities to walk away from the challenge. Many times, we hyper focus on why and how we can stop instead of figuring out why or how we can continue. It might even be part of our natural instinctual programming to avoid challenge and pain. However, each time you do that, you rob yourself of vital information about your own capabilities. You risk limiting yourself because you never get to unleash your own potential. Each time you step away from a challenge for the right reason, you have failed that challenge for the wrong one. My mind was set. I was pushing on. The Old Man on my back grins in the mirror as I turn away to go pack my gear up. I have pavement to pound and miles to make up, so let me organize my shit and make my next move.

An internal switch had clicked inside me that morning. I don't think I recognized it at that point. I lay all my gear out strategically. All my tank bag items are lined up on the hotel room desk. All my rucksack items are pulled out and laid out on the left side of the bed. All the shit in all my pockets is laid out on the right side. I take a mental inventory of everything then reorder their location sensibly as I pack. I am anticipating encountering obstacles now, so I am thinking ahead and preparing. I'm focused. Almost subconsciously, I'm rolling up all my clothes items in tight small rolls like I was first taught in boot camp. I pack up all my gear and suit up.

It is common outlaw protocol and basic Outcast respect not to smother The Old Man. That means no items go over him. When riding in a car you take your cut off for this reason. You don't put a coat over him. There are extenuating circumstances that you reverse him so he touches you and not whatever you put on. Given that I am traveling with the black rucksack strapped to my back, I am not going to disrespect The Old Man. I slowly fold the vest up and gently place it as the last item in my rucksack. I recognize now how symbolic that action was to the internal switch that clicked that morning, but I had no clue then. It solidified the transition in roles that just happened. The *biker* got us here and is pushing us and has the network that is making this all possible. The *soldier* is going to take this leg now. He is going to carry us through to our next checkpoint on this mission. They are an evolving duality dependent on each other's counterforce. I look in the mirror, and the soldier in me looked back. He looked at me with his half-skull mask over his head reversed so only the black showed, black goggles, black leather coat, black cargo pants, tightly laced black tactical boots, black survival cord handle Benchmade attached to the small of his back underneath the black military rucksack. (X-Ray this is Night Wolf, all systems green, one vic, one pack, requesting SP time: now).

I march out of the hotel room and downstairs. I walk around to the motorcycle. There is a new energy in the air. Even the bike has a new attitude this morning. It looks different, with no saddlebags on it, and how it's leaning toward me. It does not look like the cliché representation of what a member of an outlaw motorcycle club's motorcycle would look like right now. It looks more aggressive this morning, but humble. It looks like a 1600cc Outcast Attack Cycle (OAC). I walk up to it and man the vehicle. It rumbles to life ready to be activated. I tap in the coordinates to Walmart in my GPS and rip off toward that location. I get there quickly. I park the OAC, and almost with the intensity of clearing a building, I breach the store's perimeter and head to Customer Service. I fill out the paperwork. Black Ice sends the challenge and password. The teller challenges me with a phrase. At Walmart, when you do a transfer, there is a password-related phrase that the sender gives and a response that the receiver should know as a security measure. I respond with the password agreed upon by Black Ice and me. The transaction is accepted. I have the funds. I decide to purchase a prepaid MasterCard on which to put most of the cash I just received, so I don't lose the money given that I don't have a wallet anymore. I pay for the card and have the teller load it with most of the money I just received. She does. I immediately dial the activation number on the back to activate the card. I am walked through automated instructions and eventually get to a point where I am asked to enter the card number. I do. Nothing happens. I stay on the line for a solid ten minutes before attempting to activate the card again. The exact same thing happens. I make another unsuccessful attempt before I call back and navigate the automated menus to a card-services repre-sentative. I explain the situation in detail to the representative and ask her to activate the card. After a series of nonsensical questions about what state I live in and other random topics, she tells me possibly the card is defective. I'm unsure if even *she* believes the resolve she just told me. After a total of about twenty-five minutes on the phone, the only solution that card-services can offer is that they mail me a duplicate card to my house. I'm currently in Kentucky. I live in Massachusetts. That will not help me at all. I literally felt like a JG Wentworth commercial: "It's my money, and I want it now!" I go back up to the teller and ask her to refund the card and just give me the cash back. This is impossible, she assures me. She tells me there is nothing she can do once the money has been put on the card. Then, she suggests I call the number that I had just been on the phone with for twenty-five minutes. So in summary, I just got funded money to continue this trip and, in a matter of minutes, I potentially just locked it all away on a card. For which I will have to get a duplicate mailed. To a location I am not in. Wow! The creative ways I'm being challenged are almost humorous now.

As much as my mind has been anticipating various obstacles and preparing for them now, I must admit I never saw anything close to this one coming. I was almost numb at this point. I was very much annoyed but surprisingly not angry. I just have to figure out a solution. I'm pacing up and down the aisles trying to come up with something, but I really don't know what to do right now. I can't ask the club to fund me another stack of money minutes after they just sent me money. Even if they somehow agree to do that, it is going to take some time for Black Ice to get it and do what he just did all over again. I'm thinking to myself how I should have just kept the cold-hard cash instead of fucking with that damned card. I can easily see cash like that falling out of one of my pockets during a rest stop or something. I'm still pacing back and forth in front of Customer-Care, thinking maybe I should have just bought a wallet instead of the card, when the teller calls out to me and says, "The only other option I can think of is to try online." I respond, "Yeah? Do you have online access in here?" Of course not. I pull out my smartphone, sit on the bench, pull the card out, and give it a shot. There is no mobile app so I have to navigate webpages on the phone as if they are on a computer. I pull up the page. Try to expand it with my fingers and input all the information it is asking me for. There is a box that asks me to enter the card number. I enter the digits carefully and tap the screen finalizing my entry. The screen goes blank. I look over at the teller. She must have been able to feel my frustration, because she already had a face of consolation as she looked back at me. I glanced back at the white screen right as it changed, and the words "Card Activated" appeared. I lay back against the bench, let out a sigh of relief and try to get my motivation back. I snap out of it. Next plan of action is to get some food and re-establish communication with my point of contact in Kansas City.

I'm in a Super Walmart with a whole grocery store in it, but I decide to get a meal from the pre-cooked, hot foods section. Of course, the aggravation continues. No worries though. It's not even worth going into detail, but I genuinely don't understand the logic in having someone who speaks no English try and serve food at an establishment where the majority of the customers speak English. Don't get me wrong, I have a grandmother who is sharp as a knife but probably only knows English about twenty percent. This is *not* what I'm talking about. I am describing someone who speaks absolutely *no* English. They might be able to say "Monday" or "Tuesday" on a fucking leap year but other than that, nothing. Then they have a boss attempting to assist by yelling at them in English completely different shit than what I am even asking them for. Sigh... no anger. I got something to eat. Not at all what I was asking for but something nonetheless. Next step is to contact Big June and Mayday in Missouri and get back on

67

the road. I establish comms with Mayday who tells me the chapter president, Big June, will meet me when I get there. I eat silently outside on a bench. I man my OAC. I'm gone.

It was back in 2000, in this very state of Kentucky, that I was initiated into the United States Army as a wolf in 1/46th "Wolfpack" Infantry by ways of Fort Knox. Here I am, again, as a wolf in a completely separate Wolf Pack of Afghanistan today. It was here, almost two decades ago, I had an olive drab rucksack humping it over hills named Misery, Agony, and Heartbreak. Here I am, today, with that very same rucksack, just in black, humping it down these deserted highways with names unknown to me. It was here, all those years ago, I realized I had made a decision to join an organization that would affect me for the rest of my life. Here I am, again, realizing that I have made another decision to join an organization that is going to ask of my dedication for the rest of my life. The comparison of then to now was impactful. The parallels between that life and this one are screaming out during this journey.

I remember being a young private, at Fort Knox, and having that internal switch kick on. Other soldiers would rally and wait for mail call. They would take the push-up penalty for receiving mail with a smile. *Anything* to hear from home. I, on the other hand, asked my family not to contact me, and I would be in the back of the bay doing pushups on my own for every piece of mail other soldiers received. I guess I was focused on trying my best to become the soldier I was being molded into.

Here I am, breathing that same Kentucky air, and that solemn mode has taken over once more. It was not too long ago I was communicating with Three and Grass. I was shooting texts out to bros at gas stops and joking. It all dissipated. It's not even voluntary or something that I am aware of when it happens. It is just a switch that clicks, and when it does, I am in performance mode. I am void of emotions. I am void of obligations to anyone outside of the mission parameters. I have little concern for comfort. I do not register any of this. I switch into a robotic, terminator-like, projection of myself, and I move. My motorcycle was not a cruiser anymore. It had rid itself of that responsibility almost instinctively knowing we had to be streamlined for this mission. How I rode the machine now reflected the transition as well. We had switched to "Attack Posture". I crouched in, leaned over her tank, perfectly shaped to receive me. The strip of metal spikes on my helmet continued right where the sport-windshield on the front of the machine left off. I loosened the straps of the ruck so it hung low and sat almost connected to the seat of the bike. My elbows rested on the corners of her fuel tank and my knees sat just under the sides. We were fused. A half man, half machine force on the hunt. My vision was tunneled. I did not see highway signs. I did not see scenery. I saw road and obstacles in the road that we attacked. My mind would compute information on the road as data being inputted into the machine: Green vehicle, middle lane, 300 meters... 200 meters...100 meters, passed. Two vehicles, left lane and right lane, passage point created, passing. Everything was methodic, and information flowed through my brain almost subconsciously. Speed 100mph... 110mph... curve ahead, large truck middle lane, 120mph... road kill, lane shift. I was moving. The weather seemed to match my mode. The clear skies became darker. Ominous clouds rolled over each other anxiously overhead. The sky exploded with lightning accompanied by heavy rain. The windshield decreased visibility by 10%... heavy rain decreased it by 15%... tinted goggles decreased visibility by 3%... My mind continued to compute data. Total visibility decreased by 28%. Final calculation: Push on. My OAC and I whizzed through the rain. A storm is a storm. My OAC and I attacked that storm.

HOOD LODO

Some people will ground themselves and wait a storm out. I understand. Some storms you just have to do that. What I have learned from this trek is that most of them you can just attack. You move faster than the storm, so you can wait around for six hours and go get something to eat and do all that bullshit waiting for the shit to stop, or you can attack. You might be cutting right through the heart of the storm and deal with misery for quite some time but like all the storms in life, eventually it ends. Sooner or later the sky has to turn light blue again and when it does, you did it. You ate that storm. I speed on, storm attacked, cars attacked, trucks attacked. I'm attacking everything.

Suddenly, I get a sensation that pops me up from underneath my windshield. I snap out of Attack Posture as if I hit one of those big-ass bugs that nails you in the center of your forehead, right under your helmet (it happens to all of us). However, it's not a bug. It's like a sixth sense that makes you pop up very alert, like a dog responding to a dog whistle. It's an instinct. I realize my instinct was a little too late in this scenario as I fly by and, as if it were in slow motion, watch the State Trooper target lock on me. He tears out onto the highway from his little cove and chases behind me. He throws his lights on when I change lanes. I look at my fuel. I look at what model cruiser he is in. I calculate when the next exit is and my odds at burning this cop if I slam full throttle. I compute that data. I pull over. Damn!

Truthfully, I had a fucking good stretch with no "fuzz". (I might be the only person I know that still calls cops "the fuzz". This is a term well before my time. I think I came across it in the book *The Outsiders* when I was in grade school. It stuck. So, in addition to all the other terms for cops, I re-introduce "the fuzz". See, now you learned something.) "Ok, fuzz-bucket, let's do this," I say. I shut the bike off, take my helmet off, and rest my head on my arms over the tank as I wait for Porky to walk up. I can hear him strolling up to me in the gravel on the side of the road. The sound the gravel is making as he approaches sounds like crushed bacon bits. A calm, almost gentle voice asks, "You gotta license?" These cops are throwing me the fuck off out here. You know how you have come to just expect that typical fuck-you, antagonistic, tone in their voice when they address you? He did not have that tone at all. He simply asked me for a license as if he was asking me to borrow a pen. "I don't have one." I might as well run down the story now. I chuckle at the true story I'm about to tell him because how ridiculous it is going to sound, "See, I lost my wallet back in Ohio. I have a lost property report number for it." I give him a piece of paper with a series of numbers written down on it and a name. I continue, "I'm riding across the country and it has just been situation after situation. My plates tore off. I lost my military IDs and license." He interjects, very interested, with, "Where are you coming from?" I reply, "Massachusetts." He laughs, impressed. "You're a long ways from home! Wait, you rode all the way from Massachusetts?" "I did," I say. He continues asking me where I'm going but is still stuck on the fact I rode all the way to Kentucky from Massachusetts. He asks for my registration, which I give him, and he tells me, "You were doing well over a hundred back there." Maybe he was looking for me to insert some type of explanation, because he paused after saying that. I had nothing to say. He walks back to his cruiser.

Moments later I hear him approaching me again. I scope him out in my side mirrors. He lays it on me, "I gave you a break on the speeding. I did put it in that I warned you about not displaying a license plate." I'm flabbergasted! "I'm going to pull out and block traffic for you as you pull off. You be safe." "Thank you. I appreciate that." I suit up quickly and take off on the OAC. These police officers out here are, like, blowing my mind! That shit would never have gone down like that on a Massachusetts highway. Those state troopers, not all of them but definitely most of them, would have fucking

71

nailed me to the cross for no tail light, no license plate, speeding, etc. They would have played the whole "Handcuff you for both of our safety" thing, slammed me for the knife. It would have been terrible. That military shit would not have had any worth either. Most of them are military themselves and they will fuck military over just the same (sometimes worse). This dude was being real fucking decent. I respect that.

Back to beating up this pavement. Now, let me explain something. Besides the desolate routes in the deserts of Iraq, or the sand-dusted landscapes of Kuwait, I have never seen roads like those in Midwestern America. I have never before ventured into the purity of the plains that permeate this humble setting. Never have I taken the opportunity to see these roads completely enshrouded in calmness. Serenaded by the song sung from the four stroke, V-twin 1600cc displaced, liquid cooled personification of freedom that has created a merger with my being on this journey, I become one with my new-found environment. I become a newly featured image in the romantic imagery of American representation. Those commercials that displayed the open road with a lightly clothed white male on his motorcycle with the horizon in front of him has been modified by me. This is no commercial. This is no poetic ending to a culture changing movie or a fantastic television series solidifying the imagery we subconsciously accept of what freedom means for some. This is real life. This is that exact beautiful projection enhanced with an all-black motorcycle, married to an all-black clad *black* male. Not a man with the cliché, farmland history he exudes as he rides within this setting, but by a black man who represents a different economic and social background. A black man who carries a piece of the hood with him. The horizon is penetrated by the black silhouette of a black man that carries every level of bravery, boldness, and balls that the ancestry of the black people who perished during the creation of these forgotten roads carried with them. As foreign to him as it was foreign to them, he travels. I travel. I explore, with wide eyes, a nation in the name of which I have fought but whose name I have not ever taken the opportunity to explore. Simplification similar to the serenity only the deepest deserts can offer lays to the left and right of me pierced only by the road of which solely I am a guest. I am gifted with an endless straightaway of road that would unlock any seed of outlaw spirit in any biker. There is only the bike, the biker, and the road. At this moment, nothing else matters. No laws, no police, no inhibition. I increase the throttle. The engine sound is harmonized by the wind in my ears. My thoughts transcend into a combination of enhanced awareness and nostalgic daydreaming. Memories of the wind in my face as I manned machine gun turrets racing through the roads in Iraq seeped into my thoughts. The sensation of un-familiarity was so familiar. I continue to increase the throttle. The orchestra of whipping wind and roaring engine is joined by the rattle from my leather coat collar vibrating rapidly against my neck like a hi-hat. I submerge in the crescendo of road sounds and vibe out.

I'm very much in the zone. The white lane lines in the road flash past me so rapidly they appear like a fading solid line. They are the violin strings I play as I slide from note to note on this instrument road. I closed my eyes and tuned into the deafening symphony of wind, engine, dust, and leather. It was amazingly orchestral. There was no more throttle to give. I was dancing on the redline of my engine's last gear. She was at her climax. I could hear in the height of this music a new instrument introducing itself into the orchestra. I listened closer to the soft, but growing, tone. I was so deep in the zone it was euphoric. This new tone grew louder as it danced down a note then raised back up a note. I couldn't place my finger on its source. It gradually grew louder commanding more of my attention. It was alarmingly louder and was causing discord amongst

73

my other instruments. The tone grew louder still and transformed from an addition to the sweet orchestra to an annoying instrument trying to force a solo.

I snapped out of my zone. The wind was raping my face. Bugs were meeting their death on my nose. Speckles of sand peppered my cheeks and all my senses were back on full alert. I opened my eyes. The sounds were no longer instruments. The wind was yelling at me. The engine was roaring at me. My leather jacket was rapidly tapping me as if it wanted attention. The tone was no longer an instrument either as it wailed at me. It was that familiar sound, and my side mirror confirmed it. Right above the "objects are closer than they appear" sticker was the flashing red and blue lights of a state police cruiser. Fuck! I was literally going as fast as the motorcycle could go, and I have no idea how long he was behind me. This motherfucker is damn near inside my exhaust pipe he is so close to me. Fuck! I don't even want to hit the brake because I don't have a brake light and don't want him to hit me. He is that close to me. I release the throttle and trail off in speed toward the side of the road. I rumble over the rumble strip and stop the motorcycle. Here we go again. I take my helmet off, pull the gloves off and pull that piece of paper with the numbers on it and name ready to run down my spiel. *Crunch, crunch, crunch* the sound of bacon bits gets louder. "Turn the engine off," he barks. Sigh... He has that tone that I'm familiar with from cops on the East Coast. "License and registration," he says.

Maybe I should explain to you all here that about two weeks before this trek I had to go to the Defensive Driver's Course for the third time. That's the mandatory weekend course you have to go to when you get too many tickets. If I get one more surchargeable offense my license gets suspended for sixty days. I have a highly decorated driving record. So, this is not good. Not at all. Porky is not giving me that good vibe either. I need to get the story out before he goes back to the cruiser. Anyway, I give him my license and registration. "The bike yours?" he asks. "Yes." I start to run down the story but don't even get a word out. "Where's the plate?" he interrupts. I tell him it tore off. Almost disgusted, he turns and starts to walk back to his cruiser right after telling me he pulled me over for speeding. I watch him get in the cruiser and close the door. I watch him in my side mirror typing away on his laptop. I'm sure he is running my license number now and reading my novel of a driving record. My eyes are glued to him. I'm peering at him through his windshield, trying to see if I can read his facial expressions if he makes any. He doesn't. I'm staring, attempting to see him actually write the citation. He doesn't seem to do anything but sit in the cruiser slightly leaned towards the laptop. He definitely did not write anything down when I saw the cruiser door open again. He marches toward me. I scan his hands looking for that small, flimsy, white citation form I'm so used to. I don't see it. This could be a good thing. The way these midwestern police seem to have a more reasonable approach than the east coast ones, this might go well. In the event he wants to talk to me about something else, I start preparing my story in my head. I really need to sell it the way I sold it last time. He walks up, and I turn to run down the whole series of issues I have run into during this trip, and how I'm a vet trying to explore my own country as opposed to all the ones I've been in. I turn right into his outreached hand. My shoulder hits and crumples a full-sized sheet of paper he is extending toward me. Apparently, this state trooper has a cruiser that prints out 8.5"x11" tickets, which is not anything I have seen before. "You have twenty days to appeal the ticket," he says icily. I actually asked this dude if there is a way I can fight this ticket without having to come back to the state of Kentucky. He looked at me like I had six heads and proceeded to tell me that he tagged me with the radar gun, plus he pursued me well above the speed limit and confirmed by pacing me when he caught up to me. I said nothing. I stuffed the ticket in the tank bag as he walked back to his cruiser.

I don't even turn my bike on yet. I don't want this cop behind me, and I just want to process how that ticket might affect me. I'm unsure how connected these systems are now that the Patriot Acts and other acts have crossbred state and federal law and systems. I don't know how, or if, I am going to have a suspended license from this. I don't remember how long it takes to suspend the license and question whether my license will be active for the remaining portion of this trip. If I get pulled over again, and my license is suspended, shit is really going to be fucked up then! I also am thinking ain't no way in hell I'm coming back to Kentucky for anything court-related. I can promise you that. I power on the bike, helmet on, gloves on, and I take off once more.

I blew out of Kentucky. After that cop I pretty much didn't see any more at all for hours. I was blowing through Missouri, and all was good until I hit the ridiculous traffic in St. Louis. First of all, it's as hot as two devils fucking on a brimstone mattress. Secondly, people drive like they don't give a fuck. I don't give a fuck either, so it's a bad combination. Usually I would just jump out of traffic and blaze through the breakdown lane, but I was in it today. These foreign, urban, highways get tricky, so I didn't want my GPS to tell me to take a left lane exit while the road splits, and I am way over on the right. It was not a long distance that I was in traffic, but St. Louis has traffic at the level of Boston. That's all I have to say about that shit. If we still had a clubhouse out here, I would have hit that shit.

I reach Kansas City at nightfall. I'm just pounding through towns. I'm almost at the clubhouse. Yeah, all that shit about not seeing cops... You can toss that away, 'cause the minute I hit Kansas City, cops are everywhere. That's the first sign I'm in the hood. I pull out of the gas station and I'm at the intersection with a local cop. With no plate and no taillight, I'm really hoping his light turns green before mine does because cops in the hood can go two ways: either they find any reason to fuck with you so a taillight is a perfect reason, or they are so bloodthirsty for drugs and guns that they see someone with a missing tail light and don't even bother. Of course, I get the green light. Fuck it, I push through. Whatever happens is going to happen. He didn't light me up immediately, so he wasn't going to. As I slide down this street and that street, getting deeper and deeper, I absorb the energy of this hood. The familiar scent of poverty looms over the unfamiliar sights I pass by. I submerge myself in the vibe of Kansas City.

I allow the tone of the hood to dictate my mode. There is a unique voice spoken by the streets of this hood. There is a stillness very different from the busy night life in other hoods. It's the type of neighborhood you can't hide in. I roll slowly through streets absorbing the dudes on corners. They look at me and assess me. I look at them and assess them. An unspoken instinctual language is mutually communicated and it's either a problem or it's not. A language that is based on the energy you project. I'm very familiar with this language but not familiar with this city. It's eerily quiet. The east coast hoods buzz at night and get very active. This is different. Not many people are out at all. Police are patrolling hard. I see them. They hear me. My mode makes me a seen shadow. I'm noticed but have the energy of someone who, simultaneously, is not to be fucked with but also not threatening. It's an energy I project because it is a true energy. All hoods have a universal unspoken language that permeates their residents. This language becomes fluent by experience only. To those unfamiliar it's extremely confusing and misdirected. But to those that are familiar, it's a second nature that involves the maximum capacities of your senses. You learn to discern fear and posturing versus solidness and hardness. To many, it looks the same. To those that can discern, it is the difference between hunted and hunter. To those who speak the language, they can walk up to a squad of hunters, socialize, and keep it moving. Hunters recognize hunters. To those who don't have the language, they might put the wrong signals out and have the wrong energy and cause tension everywhere they move.

The fact of the matter is there is a seriousness to every hood that makes the very natural and important codes relevant. We have strayed as a "developed" society that allows compensations for the code of nature. In our developed society a weak, fearful person can hide those flaws behind false projections of strength. Weakness can be masked by social acceptance because of wealth, or manmade gauges of intelligence. Characteristics that are unacceptable by the laws of nature can be pacified by created definitions of strength, courage, or morality. In the hood – any hood – there is a byproduct that exists from the fact that the hood is rejected by this created social structure. It's a two-part equation. Primarily, you get those who fight with every fiber of their energy to try and merge with the created structure. They gauge their self-value off of the structure that already has rejected them. It's an endless, uphill battle. Secondly, there are those who cognize that being rejected from the created structure forces them to be in tune with the code that has existed before every man-made code, the natural code. There are those who, either by choice or circumstance, speak another language, a natural language, where you can't hide your weaknesses. You have no choice but to face your fear. You either get strong, get smart, get wise, get hard, get real, or get conquered. It forces a resilient character, or it exposes a weak character. Either way, it is real. This language of realness is what those that did not have the opportunity to learn the language fight their whole lives, despite the luxuries of the created structure, to learn. They are never given *real* opportunities to assess their strength because their value of self comes from a non-natural scale.

My contemplations on this sociology are interrupted by my GPS telling me my destination is up ahead. I slowly roll up to the clubhouse, which has an image of The Old Man outside to let me know I'm home. The clubhouse is dead quiet. The street is dead quiet. I pull out my phone and call Mayday to let him know no I'm at the clubhouse. He tells me he is two hours away, and he is going to hit me right back. He calls me back, minutes later, and tells me Big June fell out and will be there in ten minutes. I hang up and park my bike on the sidewalk under the large Outcast symbol on the window. I open my rucksack and pull The Old Man out. I'm on my post. I circle the building in stealth just to get an awareness of my surroundings. That still energy makes me want to slip into the shadows, so I do and observe the block from the shadow cast by the clubhouse staircase. I crack a half pint of Jacks I picked up somewhere before I rolled into Kansas City.

The night is so still it's tense. I see no vehicles driving by. I hear very few sounds besides the breeze in the warm air. I take another swig of the Jacks. It's as warm as the air around me. I could feel it before I could hear it. I could hear it before I could see it. The stillness is broken by a vehicle creeping toward the intersection. I don't suspect it is June because it's too soon for him to have gotten the call, woken up, got loaded up, and be down here from wherever he is coming from. I watch the vehicle pull up slowly; I watch as it stays a few seconds longer than it needs to before it starts to roll through. There is no question that their attention is on me. My attention is on them. We are the only living creatures out here it seems. I slowly slip my hand in my duster. I don't feel the threat yet, but by the way this trip is allowing everything to go wrong, I would not be surprised if I get into a shootout in the middle of Kansas City. I have perfect cover because the staircase is protected by a stone wall and raised earth. I could easily rise right over the wall and have a platform to let off well-placed shots without being exposed or even seen. I'm watching the vehicle. It's pretty much stalled in the middle of the street. The tension is undeniable at this point. Fuck it, I come out of the shadows calm and ready. The vehicle still creeps. It pulls to the side. I'm ready for whatever they want. I see a female get out. She doesn't look over at me. She doesn't cross the street either. As I said before, there is nothing but stone wall holding in the raised earth on this side. She is going to come to me. She does. This is my first time in this city, and I control the energy around me, which is in shadow mode, so I can't see what the reasoning would be for anyone to come and talk to me right now. Unless she is looking for some rocks, pills, or whatever drug is popping out here. Why the fuck would she get out of the truck for that. These questions are running through my mind as I watch her walk up. I'm still calm, and all is good so far. If she acts stupid that's another story. I have a bottle of Jacks in one hand, and beneath my coat, I have something else in the other. Either she came for peace or she came for the piece. Either way, I got whatever it is she's looking for.

She reaches me, and she speaks, "Hey?" She is hesitant, not loud, not confident, but not scared. She continues, "I'm Bubbles, Property of Big June." Oh, ok. I introduce myself and give her a hug. "Where the fuck's he at?" I pass her the bottle, and we start talking. She relaxes. Bubbles seems cool as shit. It does not take long to see that. I have a habit of asking POs what it means to them to be a PO. I gather a lot of information about them and their sponsors as they answer the question. Bubbles gives me her run down. She starts off with the resounding number one answer, "Take care of your sponsor." She goes into more personal detail afterward. We talk for a bit. I ask her, "What benefit does she get from being a PO?" another question I tend to ask POs. I think I threw her off with this question for a quick second, but she recovered easily and gave me her answer. At that moment, here enters that motherfucker Big June. We slap hands, hug, and all that Outcast shit. He sounds like he just woke up, "You rode all the way up here on that?" He already knows the answer and doesn't even wait for my response as he mumbles his signature phrase, "Well, goddamn."

We walk up the stairs and he opens one of the doors to the clubhouse. I walk in that bitch and inhale deeply. Yup, it feels like Outcast in that bitch. Certain clubhouses have a certain feel to them. The same feel that if you bring certain chicks that are not built for this life into you can see it on their face they won't make it. Kansas City has that Outcast energy to it. I'm in the clubhouse running down answers to questions about my trek and all the bullshit. June is entertained by the shit. Bubbles brings me a beer and slips into the corner. I'm happy to be here. I'm in and out of my rucksack, but it's like I'm not really doing anything. I'm unpacking things and packing things. June is chilling while I pace back and forth telling my story all animated. I think I'm just happy to be off the road right now. I'm ready to decompress.

Before June gives me a tour of the clubhouse, he gives me a bottle of white shoe polish. It's tradition to scribe your name on the black walls of Outcasts clubhouses. I won't put my name on the wall of any clubhouse unless I have made the ride on iron. I take my time and place my artistic representation of myself on the wall. Then I take the tour of the clubhouse's upper and lower levels. They have a good setup in Kansas City. "So what you wanna do?" June asks. He is trying to feel me out and host me. He continues, "You trying to go out or...?" I'd rather just hang with my bro and learn who the fuck he is. "Nah, I'm not with all that. We chilling, bro," I say. He responds, "Well goddamn." I pass June a beer, and we go back outside and sit on the bench outside of the stone wall.

HOOD LODO

You would think, because of the time I arrived, that I would talk for about an hour then go to sleep. It was late, and I was tired, but June and I just keep talking. We get into a conversation about Outcast and his vision for the organization. I share my perspective. I'm very passionate and June is matching my passion level as we talk and laugh. I feel this dude. He connects with me as well. As we are talking, another female pulls up who I assume is another property of June. She greets him. He waits a minute then he reprimands her quickly for not greeting me. She does. I don't remember her name. June asks me if I want something to eat but he is already huddling up with his POs, putting a plan together before I even answer. He has Bubbles and the other property roll out to get me two pounds of gizzards. They take off together while June and I continue talking.

They come back with the gizzards. I don't eat this shit on the East Coast much. I'm curious to be reminded of what gizzards taste like. Part of what I enjoy most about being out of town, state, or country is experiencing what the residents experience. I eat what they eat. I see what they see. I get involved and I enjoy it, or I don't, but I experience it firsthand. I don't even know what they forgot to put in the box, but Bubbles asks me, dead seriously, if I wanted her to take it back. It was the smallest thing, but she was resolved, damn near taking it out of my hand. The two POs were gone with the food to go and take care of whatever was missing. It could have been sauce. It could have been that there was not enough, or it was cooked the wrong way. I have no clue. I just let them execute whatever June asked them to. I watched. You can tell Bubbles is groomed well as a PO. She stands out amongst some of the POs I have met. They return minutes later with a fresh, steaming box of food.

We are back to talking, agreeing, disagreeing, and laughing. We are only interrupted by Bubbles bringing me beers periodically and taking away my empty cans.

Without exposing what June and I spoke about, because it was hours of Cast business, I can tell you this: Big June is another one of those selected few that I connect with. I dig that dude. He continually tells me I'm one of the rare ones. I'm not sure completely what he means by it, but by some of the topics we discussed, I have an idea. I feel the same about him. We have a lot of similar views on certain things. So, pounds of gizzards, a lot of laughter, getting loud, and empty beer cans later, I'm ready to take it in and sleep. June makes sure I'm all set and know where everything is if I need it. Bubbles makes sure I'm good and don't need anything now. I assure them again, and again, that I'm all set and will be more than fine. There is no sexy shit to sleep on, but that is not a prerequisite for Outcast. I have beer if I need it, water, a bathroom, my duster, shelter, and my motorcycle outside. I'm a more than happy man.

I pull out the broken convertible couch and throw some extra cushions on it. Before June leaves he slaps something in my hand and says, "This is your house." I look down in my hand, and there is a key in it. That gesture, no matter what the context, has so much impact on me. It is such a display of trust. Whenever someone puts a key in your hand, for anything, it says a lot without saying anything. I nod and look him in his eyes. With silent words I tell him what he already knows. I tell him I will forever respect and defend this property of ours without ever opening my mouth. I give my bro a hug and lock up after him. I place my weapon on the cushions, pull my duster over me, and settle into my hide.

I lay there in silence. Topics about what June and I spoke on and how this all unfolded replay in my head. Although this trip is full of bullshit, I'm starting to appreciate some of the good shit that is happening as well. If I had rolled with other bros, June and I would not have had the conversation we had. We probably would have never met until much later. I don't know if the other group went to any clubhouses at all. They may have just pushed straight to California and stayed at hotels and motels. I'm starting to appreciate my path. I have gotten connected with a lot of bros and have bros checking on me and texting me which really adds another dynamic to it. There is a nation of brothers out there. It feels good to connect with them. Come out to their house, crack a brew with them, eat some food together, bond, and get a feel for what cloth they are. If it's family, then that's what family does. I looked at my vest folded up with The Old Man exposed. I'm watching over The Old Man. I let my eyes rest. They needed it. I start thinking how The Old Man's eyes never need rest. They never close. They watch my back when that vest is on me. On that note, maybe it's more like The Old Man is watching over me. I don't know. I doze off.

Day Four

The rising sun wakes me. My phone rings almost simultaneously. I clear my throat and speak, "Yo?" It's Bubbles and Big June seeing if I need breakfast. "Nah I'm good, bruh." That switch was tripped during the night, I guess. I'm back in attack mode. All I want to do is pound the shit out of the pavement. I feel recharged and motivated. I will get a snack to munch on at my first fuel stop. I make my way to one of the clubhouse refrigerators and grab a beer. I drink it as I pace around the clubhouse reading all the names of bros written in white on the black walls. I pause, looking at my name on the wall. I don't know what the feeling is but it's a solemn one. It feels good. I take the last sips of my beer when the door opens and Bubbles and June come through. June got some McMuffin sandwiches and offers them to me. I'm good I reassure him. He eats. Either he wanted cheese or didn't want cheese, but they fucked it up and Bubbles was damn near out the door to bring it back. I'm telling you Bubbles is coached well. She doesn't get all fired up and shit. It's not like she is mad or anything. She just takes the responsibility of taking care of her sponsor seriously. She wants to, and you can see and feel it. There is a standard created by Big June for his POs, and Bubbles displays it. Bang. Ok, all my lovey-dovey Kansas City shit is a wrap. Back to business. It's time to jump back on Toto and hit the yellow brick road. I start my engine, strap on my helmet, throttle up and fly off the sidewalk into the street with a middle finger in the air.

I thought Kentucky had some open roads. Apparently, I have not seen shit yet as far as what the Midwest has to offer. The yellow brick road seems to have transformed into a never-ending, desolate landing strip. Would my motorcycle and I like to tear this motherfucker up you ask? Well, don't mind if we do! I pull my handkerchief up, tuck into attack posture, and wrench the throttle handle down. The OAC responds immediately. We are flying down the road. I have to admit the solitude is a great feeling. The plains on the left and right of me are like an ocean of land. I start to sing in the wind, "I'm a cowboy. On a steel horse I ride. I'm wanted. Waaaanted, dead or alive."

I am flying past a pasture of cows. I don't see a farm in sight. I can't help but think to myself words that Grass has mouthed to me on the road. He would drop back next to me and say some shit in the wind while nodding his head. I would struggle to read his lips and make out what the fuck he was trying to tell me. Whether I got it or not did not matter. He would say it, and then throttle up back into the formation. Now I find myself saying it: "I love this shit." There is not a vehicle in front, or behind me for as far as I can see. I am alone and loving it. It's meditative. It's a sense of freedom and isolation that is liberating. This is the feeling I would chase at night in Afghanistan when it felt like everyone was asleep except me. This is that unique tranquility that I would receive under the stars in the dead quiet of the remote deserts of Iraq. It's a temporary escape from everything. It's a brief moment when you can simply *be* the moment. You are not capturing it. You are not altering it. You are not controlling it. You are just *it*. This experience has such a euphoric calm to it that, once you experience it, you will probably chase it for the rest of your life. You will need your fix of tranquility, and you will have to find it. You will realize that there are tranquility dealers all around you. I'm not talking about that poorly cut with procaine version of tranquility we try to get. I mean that pure uncut meditative state of tranquility you find in little pockets of nature that are all around you, those little havens that allow you to recharge and face any obstacle in front of your spiritual growth. You might find one on an empty beach. You might find one in a park so early in the morning that the joggers aren't even out yet. You might find one deep in that forested area on the side of the road that you drive by every day. They are all around you. It does not require expensive retreats and planned vacations. It requires the bravery to slip out of the chains real quick and just go to them. They are there for you. They are there for us. Here in the Midwest, as I torpedo down this desolate interstate, and the earth rotates around making the sun appear like it is exhausted and leaving, I think I found one. I slowly release the throttle of the OAC and coast to a slow roll on the side of the road. I shut the engine off, close my eyes, and just breathe for a while. I dismount my iron and walk out into the field on the side of the road. I keep walking further and further into the sea of land. I don't turn back. I just continue to walk out into this ocean until I stop. I drop my rucksack, sit on the ground, lay back with the rucksack as a pillow, and decide to become *this* moment.

The OAC and I are tearing through everything. I'm getting less mileage out of my tank now than I was before. I am cruising at a much higher rate of speed though with slightly more weight. She is designed to attack. However, as sexy as all that "attack everything" stuff is, as these roads get more empty and exits are more and more spaced out, it is starting to have less and less use. Allow me to tell you a little story: So, this little bitch I know named Interstate Highway 70 West feels it is her fucking duty to highlight the fact that my OAC is designed to attack as opposed to just cruising. The motorcycle has speed but is not made for extra long distance. Not only does she feel it her duty to highlight that fact, but she also wants to remind us all that in the saddlebag that is no longer with us (pour out a little Jack Daniels for Saddlebag Left), was my two-gallon extra fuel tank that is also no longer with us. So this funky little bitch decides, somewhere leaving Kansas, that she is just going to space her fuel stops out to some ridiculous distances. She not only is going to do that, but she is going to start throwing little blue signs on the bottom of her exit signs that read "No Services" (aka, fuck you if you need fuel, food, or shelter). Oh, that bitch! The OAC and I are pushing forward because although she is scaring us, we know that she is going to produce a gas station at the last minute, right? Miles and miles later the joke is not funny anymore. I-70W, you play too fucking much. There is no fucking gas station! You can't be fucking serious! Oh wait, what is this? Is it a gas station?... No. Is it a sign for a gas station? ...No. It's a big fucking cumulus cloud that decides it's going to R. Kelly all over me and my bike! Awesome. My gloves are soaked. My outer layer is soaked. My face is soaked. Not even my New Jersey hoodie under my duster could save me from this one. That's soaked. My perimeter was breached. I felt my defenses being penetrated when that trickle of water seeped into my spine right at the base of my neck. My back was conquered. Then the worst part of being wet happens next. You feel your drawers get taken. Your balls get that chill, and your whole crotch is fucking soaked. I felt my socks and boots fill up with water. I'm officially wet from head to toe. Fuck you I-70W. Oh wait, I still have no fucking fuel! Cool. I see a rest stop sign. Fuck it. Just make it to the rest stop and I will figure the rest out from there. She huffs and puffs, and my OAC staggers into the rest stop before she is a wrap.

It is pouring even more. I dismount and dash to a little outdoor sitting area under some cover. I remove my rucksack. It feels good to take it off. I'm unsure what my next move is. I take a moment to appreciate the magnitude of this storm. It's coming down extremely hard. I run out from cover to one of few cars pulled over at the rest stop. I ask them to roll down their window. The smell of weed comes from the car as I have a brief conversation with this couple that results in nothing productive to anyone. I run back to my covered table and bench. I'm already calculating that I can pull my duster out and grab some sleep here if need be. Dusk has not hit yet, so I do not want to commit to a sleep plan while there is still light. I am going to need food and ultimately fuel. My odds are significantly higher during daylight hours, so sleeping here is not ideal. I do see a power outlet, which is critical. That changes a lot, actually. I take a moment to think. Fuck it, let's try it. I go on Google and track down the number to Highway Patrol for the state. I start making calls to any number I come across. I get nothing but machines. I leave messages, but I know I need a better plan than that. It was a shot in the dark. Maybe my only option right now is to ask every vehicle that comes in if they can help me. For some reason, I really don't think that is going to work at all. I need something more solid. I know there is an answer. I just don't know what it is right now. My phone rings. I'm not really in the mood for conversations right now. I have not been too social since I transformed into attack mode and started treating this like a true mission. I was not going to break that now especially to some number I don't know. (I heard a ghostly whisper, "Hmph..." come from the inside of my rucksack.) Sigh. I answer the phone, "Who's this?... Yes! Uh, yeah, I did call? Uh...Yeah...I'm at uh the rest stop right now on fucking I-70W... Yeah... Ok, cool." Oh shit, it was Highway Patrol! I described to them where I was, and I waited for them.

Not even twenty minutes pass by when a Dodge Charger comes rolling through the rest stop and parks right next to my bike. I walk out to the State Trooper. He greets me with, "Great weather to get stuck in, huh?!" I agree that the weather is ridiculous. He pulls a fuel canister out of his vehicle and is ready to fuel my bike up! I'm in awe. I open my fuel tank, and bang, the dude starts fueling my fucking motorcycle while giving me a weather report! "I have bad news. It's going to be like this for some days, and it's even worse further west on the interstate." I can barely pay attention to his words, 'cause I'm still in awe that I am watching a fucking State Trooper leaned over my motorcycle with a fuel nozzle that is less than a foot away from a big ass Outcast MC Old Man emblem on my windshield, fueling it up for this black, 1%er biker. This shit is blowing my fucking mind! Fuck it, "You mind if I take a picture of this?" I say to him. He responds almost gleefully, "No problem. Go for it." I dash off mumbling and chuckling to myself and grab my phone. This shit is bugging me out. I snap a few pictures, and the trooper stops posing. He was done fueling like half a minute ago. He puts the tank away and stands next to me to talk about motorcycles! He likes my motorcycle and is familiar with this model. He rides too. He finds out that I am riding across the country and our conversation continues in that direction. This State Trooper is genuinely having a full out, interested conversation with me! Not like he is asking me questions to feel me out and profile what kind of person I am. He is speaking to me like a person, and I am talking to him as a normal guy. We are joking and all that shit. He tells me how he gets a new cruiser every year and how his job is pretty sweet. I learned the charger is governed at 154mph (noted). I find out he is currently in the military as well. We start talking about our service a little bit. He was in Iraq as well. The familiarity continues. He was in the early waves, like I was. There are standard questions that veterans of this war shoot at each other. The answers don't really matter, but you just ask them for some reason. I start it off this time, "Where in Iraq were you?" I have been all over Iraq and know pretty much every base that most troops respond with when that question is asked. He responds, "This place called Ashraf." I damn near lost my shit! "Get the fuck out of here?!" was my response, verbatim. I continue, "You can't be fucking serious?! I have spoken to hundreds of troops during this war and have heard countless stories, and you might be the fifth person who has even heard of Ashraf, and the other four were lying. That's one of the places where I was," I tell him.

I guess it would only be fair to explain here that Ashraf was a secret base in existence during the beginning years of Iraq. It housed Iranian protected personnel. Although it does not exist anymore, I don't wish to go into any more detail about the facility or the mission to which it pertained. The point is that very few soldiers have ever heard of this place. I will even go so far as to express this fact: Ashraf housed a facility in the base that my mission dealt with that other units on the base in Ashraf had no idea even existed. He was there the exact same time I was there! Here I am, Hood of Outcast MC, the same dude since like maybe fourteen years old who would make it a point to give a middle finger to every cop and cop car I ever saw (and have been posted up by the cops many times for it), the same dude who had his thumb dislocated getting tackled on the run from nine cruisers, and two motorcycle units, after jumping from a roof of an establishment that was suspected of being robbed, the same dude who's been indicted, and locked up with no bail, and considered a danger to society, and a flight risk and all that shit by the cops for a double shooting, the same dude who... you get the fucking picture. This dude Hood is side by side in the rain laughing, reminiscing, and talking back and forth for about forty minutes with a State Trooper who just refueled his Outcast Attack Cycle (Mind you that in the time that we are talking about when we were both in Iraq, I was on bail! I did two tours in Iraq on bail fighting a case for a shooting. But I get sent to Iraq to shoot people. Figure that one out). You can't make this shit up! Where the fuck is a donut when you need one, 'cause I would have definitely given it to him in appreciation (ok, that was a fucked-up thing to say). Instead, I extend my hand and give the officer a firm and genuine handshake. I tell him I'm already soaked so I'm going to push on in the storm. He understands and tells me there is fuel about twelve miles west on the interstate, but if I can hold out a little further there's another place that I can get fuel and food. I nod to him in acknowledgement, rev up the OAC, and roll out into the storm. I might have tossed a middle finger up at the cop just for old times' sake.

I think it was in Kansas on I-70W that I realized the mile markers match the exits and that while heading west they count down to the state line (so much on his trip was revealing to me how much I didn't know). Because of this observation, it was no surprise when I cleared Kansas and pushed into Colorado. It was my motivator to watch the miles count down from whatever number down to one and then to be rewarded with the "Welcome to Colorful Colorado" sign. *What the fuck challenge does this state have for me?* That's how I started to penetrate state lines now. *I know it's coming. So, what you got? You states ain't broke me yet, so what's up?* Colorful Colorado got some shit up its sleeve, and I'm sure I'm going to get a dose of it. In the meantime, let me absorb some of this fucking scenery, 'cause it's *crazy* beautiful! I have seen mountains all over the place. Afghanistan is mountainous terrain. Wolfpack used to do marches "up the mountain" up and down mountains just for recon (and to drink). I have scaled mountains as a mountain warfare-trained mountaineer. I have dealt with all sorts of mountains in various contexts but Colorado's mountains, basically, blew all that shit out of the water (at least it seemed that way as I was riding through them). Every few miles is some absolutely unique series of mountains with different textures and makeup. It's May, and I'm rolling through snow covered mountains. Those switch up and turn into rolling hills, then those transform into the steepest shit you ever saw. All that straight desolate highway shit is a done deal now. The road is up, down, curves to the left, gets narrow, and all sorts of exciting transitions. It reminds me of those old arcade racing games where you go and select the difficulty of the course, and it's like: Easy (some oval track), Medium (some curvy scenic strip), Hard (Welcome to Colorful Colorado!).

So, needless to say I'm tucked in and I'm eating these curves up. The motorcycle eats curves, and when you tuck in and get low you have even more control and responsiveness from your leans. I would love to say that I was ripping through every curve scraping my foot pegs and all that sexy shit, but that was not the case. I'm whizzing by mountains that hang over my head. I'm passing signs that say, "watch out for falling rocks"! *Really? What the fuck does that...* "Ahh, fuck! Seriously?" There are little pieces of debris falling off the fucking mountains! Is that what's hot in the streets? If little pebbles are falling off mountains, I imagine these signs are alluding to the fact that large chunks of mountain fall onto the highway every so often. That might just be a bad time for someone in a car, but for people on motorcycles, that could definitely be fatal. Awesome. It used to be me riding through the sunset like a Hallmark card. Then the storm beat me up. The sun used to be visible but that little fucker abandoned me about seven mountain stacks ago. It's not fully dark but it's getting there. I have been riding hard all day and still seem to be chasing my time hacks. Colorado, because of its terrain, requires you to pay attention to its service stations because they are unpredictable. I have decided to just hit anything I see once I clear eighty miles on my odometer. I keep pushing.

As sunlight dissipates it's like the course gets crazier and crazier. The road turns into miles and miles of pavement surrounded by mountain that turns into bridges bordered by cliffs. Then, for no visual reason, it just completely cuts off all lanes but one, and turns into miles of orange construction barrels. I don't even understand how you get construction equipment up here! There is no breakdown lane at all. There is road that now is just cutting into mountains and turning into tunnels. If you breakdown

93

on this stretch of road, you are fucked. You are seriously fucked. I'm thinking about this shit and hoping very sincerely that this is not the trick Colorado has up its sleeve for me. I want you to imagine a single lane of twisting highway that is so entrenched in mountain that there is no space for a breakdown lane. There are obviously no street signs, because you cannot run power lines in mountain. There is no sunlight and barely any signage. If you breakdown, you will block the entire road, and you just have to hope that a vehicle doesn't fly around a mountain curve and nail you. I don't even know how a tow truck or rescue vehicle would help you. I really don't. These fucking mirror-tinted amber lenses can eat a fucking dick right now because that mirroring is impeding the little bit of visibility I have. I'm finding myself raising my goggles to try and see in this crazy terrain. Even after I buy clear glasses at a fuel stop and ride with those, the terrain Colorado is dishing out gets worse and worse.

I see now that this, alone, might be the trick up Colorado's sleeve. The course is fucking dangerous in the day. But, alone at night, it is just too much for me. I'm tired. I have been running hard all day and night. I'm still wet from the storm in Kansas, and the mountains are fucking cold! They are extremely cold! It's deep into the nighttime, and I flash around one curve of road that is so sharp that I raise up out of my tuck, shaking my head, and talking out loud to myself that I'm done. I tap out. I am not doing this shit anymore tonight. I need to find the next lodging spot and take it in for the night. So I carefully navigate until I find a sharp pull off that suggests there is lodging. I'm in Idaho Springs, and I find this little spot called 6 & 40 Motel, and it looks like the perfect cheap place to just crash for a few hours. I'm not looking for any amenities and shit. I really just want to get out of the cold and get some fucking rest for a few hours then get back on the road as soon as day breaks.

I roll into this dead little establishment's parking lot and dismount in front of the door. I walk in and moments later an Asian man appears. "You got vacancies?" I ask. He nods. "How much?" I ask. He said some shit like maybe forty dollars or something. I don't even fully remember. Maybe it was sixty. Whatever the price was I was willing to pay. I was done for the night. I pull out my prepaid debit card and hand it to the man. He does not take it, and he looks at me and asks, "You have ID?" *Those are the last words I want to hear formulated out of your fucking face right now, Chinaman.* (I do not know if he was from China. I do not even know if he was fully Asian. At this point, I don't fucking care. I need to sleep! So, for this story, he is Chinese. In fact, he is from Hong-fucking-Kong. It really has no relevance to the story at all.) "I don't." I stare this man in his eyes, and I am absolutely positive my facial expression is fully projecting my emotional state. We have a silent transaction of ideas. I convince him without words to take my card into a back room and return with keys. He does. "Thank you," I mumble as I push the door open. I mount the OAC and bring her a few yards down to the front door of my room. I open the door and am bombarded with that typical rancid scent. The motel looks like some D-rated movie set for some cheesy horror flick, and it has the aroma to match. It smells like body funk from a cross-country trucker with bad hygiene practices mixed with an ashtray of extinguished cigars. I have no problem with it, truthfully. I have slept in worse places.

I drop my gear, mount my OAC and ride out in search of anything to eat or a beer to crack. I find a liquor store down the street, but it is way too late in the night for it to be open. I do find a McDonald's inside a gas station. I fuel up the OAC and walk inside. Some tweaker is outside and asks me if I smoke cigarettes. "No," I respond, completely not in the fucking mood for any conversation. I purchase three cheeseburgers from McDonald's and two

HOOD LODO

40oz's of Natural Ice and a bag of Bugles from the gas station. The tweaker from outside is now inside standing next to the purchase line waiting for someone to buy cigarettes, I assume. I fucking swear if this fucking kid says another fucking word to me, asks me for a fucking dime, or anything I'm going to fucking crack him. I'm in that sort of mood right now, and your begging self is the last thing I need right now. Your existence alone and the idea of what you stand for is annoying me already. You are a beggar posted in front of the only open establishment in this little area seeking a poison you are addicted to from people also addicted to the poison. You are younger than me. Get the fuck out of my face bro, seriously. My face is saying everything you just read. Trust me. I walk outside. The tweaker said some silly shit to break my challenging stare like "Goodnight", "nice bike", or some nonsense that I brushed off. Not that I don't have a heart, but this type of interaction is far from foreign to me coming from the hood. I have given to many but have also learned the hustle. It's a hustle, plain and simple. Maybe I was being more of an asshole than I needed to be. I don't know his story and didn't stick around to ask.

I took off back to the stinky motel. I was tired, but it was still great to just relax and decompress real quick. I turned the TV on to *Commando*. Whatever. The bathroom is literally the width of the toilet. Across from the toilet is a standup shower. If you stand in the bathroom and try to spread your arms, both arms will be bent, and you will be touching both walls. It is about 3'5" wide. There is a sink in the room, randomly placed, next to the TV. I set my alarm for seven in the morning and lay down. I leave my cheeseburgers for morning. I eat a couple of Bugles and drink my beer until I knock out. (Ok, fine, I rubbed one out too. Fuck it.)

Day Five

     Seven arrives sooner than I expected. It's fine, because I got enough rest and I really want to attack the road all day today. I understand all the trek-having-some-meaning shit and all the appreciation I will have for the struggles after the fact, but I'm really not for the bullshit today. I think I'm getting mentally weathered with it all, honestly. I just want to hit my destination. Right now, the sun is up. I'm up on time. According to what I calculate, I can make it to California around 11:00 AM on Saturday. The idea is esteeming. I put on some dry clothes and dress for Colorado's cold. I suit up, lock the door to the motel, mount my motorcycle, put the key in her ignition, go to fire her up to hear her crank a few times but not start. I try again, and she cranks slower. I exhale. I try one more time and I hear a final tired crank then a rapid dull clicking. My head sinks. I sit on the machine for a moment in silence. I close my eyes. I open them back up slowly and dismount the vehicle. I just stand next to her. My riding partner just told me she can't go on. I am void of anger or any emotion. I don't have any sarcastic jokes or anything. I'm just exhausted. We did a lot. We learned a lot on this mission, but the lesson might not require us making it to California. Maybe all of this was about the heart both my machine and I showed. I don't know. I don't know anything at this point. I just stare at the machine, then stare off into the mountains for a moment before I take steps towards the motel room.

     I open the door, remove my ruck, and lay backward on the bed and just breathe. My head cannot help but think, *How the fuck am I going to get home now?* I changed my insurance before I left, so I guess I can call Progressive and have the vehicle towed to a motorcycle service shop out here. I highly doubt there is a local motorcycle repair shop in these mountains. I don't know. My funds are limited. My time is limited. I have no idea how I could stay with the machine for that amount of time, but I cannot imagine just leaving her in some state I have never been in before that is way across the fucking nation. I was so recharged when I woke up, and now I feel like just going to sleep again. I only have a few hours before I have to check out of this place. I lay back and close my eyes. I can't believe my journey is ending here. I don't even know what to do.

Then, suddenly, my eyes pop open. I raise up on the bed and stare at my rucksack. Fuck! I have an idea! I grab my duster and fish through the side pockets of the thing. In one of them is a small 10mm wrench. I grab it, throw open the door, and march out to the motorcycle. I drop to one knee and start wrenching off the bolt holding the seat on. The seat is removed and laying on the ground next to the bike. I'm already back in the room scanning for my next object of interest. I scan the walls by the door. Nothing. I scan under the window looking out to the street. Nothing. I stare at the television then push it forward and follow the cables behind the dresser it rests on. They disappear, so I grab the dresser and rip it forward, damn near dropping the television set. Bingo! Ok. I snatch the rucksack and start ripping my gear recklessly out of it. The rucksack is vomiting black socks and black briefs as I rip shit out of it. I dig my fist in, and, after finger-fucking the bottom of the bag for a few seconds, I rip my fist out, palming exactly what I was hoping I still had. In my hand is my trickle charger. I rip the TV plug out of the outlet, and plug the charger in. I walk it out to the bike, but it doesn't reach. I mount the OAC and straddle-walk her onto the sidewalk until she does reach. I plug her in and stare at what I have done. There is nothing more I can do but wait. I walk back into the motel room with the door wide open and sit on the edge of the bed with my fingers steepled under my chin. The odds are... I don't know what the odds are, but it at least feels like I'm exploring all my fucking options before my relationship with this bike takes a turn for the worse.

I guess in any relationship you want to explore all the options to make the two parties stay together. We have been through a lot. I do not want us to separate like this. Not here in Colorado. I felt defeated. Depending on how you look at it though, one could defend the fact that the trek technically did not defeat me. It wasn't as if Colorado defeated me with its insane elevation highs and lows and its treacherous roads. It wasn't that I quit. I don't even fucking know what I'm saying or thinking about at this point. I don't want to think. I just want to wait. I don't want to plan the next steps. I just want this step to work. The suspense is fucking driving me up the wall. I want to go out and check to see if she will start, but I know if I check too early I could get a false result. Honestly, I don't think I was ready to get disappointed either. I sat and waited some more. I waited about an hour and a half. Fuck it, I stood up, took a breath, and walked out to the motorcycle.

I stood next to her and eyed the whole situation starting from the cord in the wall and traced it all the way back to the bike as if I was looking for some fault I could fix to make the odds better. I placed my hand on the key, closed my eyes involuntarily, opened them, clenched my jaw, and fucking twisted. Nothing... Nothing but a slow crank. Nothing but a slow crank that turned into a chunky, voltage-energized, invigorated crank. Nothing but a chunky, invigorated, healthy, combustion initiating blast of machinery coming to life. She roared to the mountains then rumbled down to an idle. A moment later her headlight awoke, and my bitch was back. I looked at her and nodded slowly. *Welcome back. Now, let's do this.*

I walk back into the motel kind of humbled. I have to give it to you, Colorado. You are bringing out a whole new direction of challenges to me that I wouldn't have expected at all. The shit had me kind of nervous. I left my bitch on the charger so she could completely revitalize. With my new respect for Colorado's series of challenges, I feared that maybe next my cell phone gets, I don't know, missile attacked by a drone or some shit. My cellphone is my navigation system. So, as a precaution, I took this time to manually copy down all the directions from this point on to Los Angeles. I was excited but felt, kind of, uncomfortable showing it, because I have not escaped Colorado yet. That excitement somehow transferred into my necessity to hear Master P's song *Ghetto D*, which all of a sudden ingrained itself in my skull. I'm telling you the weird playlist that my subconscious DJ is playing throughout this trip has been fucking strange. So I YouTube the song and couldn't help but hop around the room rapping out loud, "First of all you gotta have nuts, don't give a fuck! See, when I bust niggas duck. They know if I miss it ain't by much!" Out of the thousands of songs that could possibly jump from my subconscious brain I would have never in eight-zillion years thought I would be hopping around rapping this one. And loving it.

I was ready to get back out on the road. I lost quite a few hours here so I'm back to attack mode. I go check my trickle charger and the solid-green light says that the OAC is revitalized and ready to perform. I bolt her back together, wrap my charger up, suit up, and lock the door. Moments after dropping the key off I am back on I-70W continuing to carve out my story in these unforgiving but magnificent mountains. I think Colorado can sense my respect for its challenges, so from this point on the state decides to just awe me with scenery. It is doing a very good job at it too. I roll past a pack of touring bikes that are just as awed as I am. They are riding significantly slower than me and absorbing the scenery as well. I join in their disorganized pack for a while but it's just too fucking square for me, and I tear out of that pack. It would make no sense to even throw a middle finger up to this kind of bikers. They would not even understand it as an outlaw thing. I'm just going to get back to rolling solo.

It seems every turn of the road is an amazing mountain view, or a strangely shaped projection looming over the road, or one of those mind-fucking, runaway-truck, emergency pull-off things. What the fuck is up with that? Let me explain these things: Ok, so you are on the downside of a windy mountain path. I assume that if a semi-trailer, or any weighty truck for that matter, loses its brakes there are pull-offs immediately next to the road that are steep, straight dirt paths up into the mountain for about maybe five hundred feet that end with a whole bunch of yellow water barrels at the top. So, let me get this shit right. You lose your brakes and are supposed to pull off up this hill and then what? Gravity is still on your ass, so I imagine you now have to manage steering this thing straight as you careen backwards down the dirt path you just flew up. I guess it's better than killing a bunch of other people. You just kill yourself. I'll take it. At least that's what I think they are for. I genuinely have no idea.

I continue through red mountains, grey mountains, green mountains, brown mountains, all sorts of mountains. The scenery is truly impressive. I find myself wondering how one would survive out here in the wilderness. How would one acquire food? What sort of animals are roving those crevices? How would one create a fire out here without carrying flint and tinder? I start having visions of taking up fighting positions in certain hides I see in the sides of the mountains.

I wonder, sometimes, if everyone thinks about shooting people as much as I do. I say that with a bit of humor because I know how alarming that sounds, but I don't mean it like that. I'm not talking about just walking around blasting people, but I think about shooting a lot. I train and have been to special courses trained on distance shooting, reading wind, studying trace, calculating distance, and the likes. Anyhow, I think of shooting people a lot. When I train, I train to kill people. It is what it is. I don't train to hit targets, or send a double lung shot through a large-racked deer. I train to kill a human being. I have personal weapons, and I train on my own to kill people. I think of that a lot. I find myself thinking about that in the mountains of Colorado. I would love to sharpen some of my engagement skills in these mountains. That's all I have to say on that.

My attack cycle and I cruise through the mountains that are starting to smooth out. It gets to the point that mile markers start to make an appearance again. I'm almost out of Colorado, and the feeling is pretty amazing. I count the miles down, tank after tank, until I reach a sign that makes me pull over. I stare at it while I'm masked up with the engine running on the side of the road. "Leaving Colorful Colorado". I look over my shoulder for oncoming traffic then throttle off past the sign. Indeed, I am leaving colorful Colorado.

"Welcome to Utah, Life Elevated". I really didn't know what the next state after Colorado was. Utah, now I know. I don't even want to ask the cocky question, "What does Utah have for me?" I'm done asking that question. I'm just trying to move quietly through these states and maybe the challenge monster won't see me. I recall being at Fort Knox, getting off that Blue-Bird bus, and from sunup to sundown was a fucking stiff-brimmed drill sergeant around every corner, just thirsting to put his foot up a private's ass. Everything you did was wrong. Everything you said was wrong. How you stood was wrong. How you talked was wrong. How you corrected how you talked was wrong. How you performed the penalty for doing something wrong was wrong. You shortly learned that you, kind of, don't want to stand out at all in boot camp. You want to blend in. Become an individual that's not an individual but part of the team.

102

That's how I wanted to move through these states right now. I just wanted to not disturb anything but absorb everything and Zen my way through. It was an admirable and smart way of thinking and moving. I think I am learning... scratch that. I think I am internalizing the meaning of being humble. I am realizing that I am stubborn sometimes. I wonder if it really takes the forces of mother nature to discipline me. I don't say that pridefully. I say that embarrassed. So, I endeavor to move quietly and un-announced through Utah.

I might be too late with this epiphany. Maybe my journey would have been less challenging if I moved with that respect through other states. I'm unsure. Now, I have come to Utah to try and blend in. Utah does not agree. Utah says, "No." Utah declares that it is the state in which you shall present yourself to be judged. There is nowhere to hide in Utah. There is nothing around you but desolation. I don't mean it like the same warm fields in Kansas. I mean the patchy, harsh, forgotten lands of Utah. It looks like the set of Mad Max, decades later, with all the people extinct. Randomly dispersed shrubs and vegetation scab the dry ground, which is sporadically interrupted by some rocky suggestion of a mountain. It seems as if portions of the mountains in Colorado had a mutinous revolt and took up angry refuge in Utah. They peer at me as I ride by. If they had mouths they would spit at me. The feeling so far was mutual.

I ride through this land amazed at how bland it is. Each fuel stop I make becomes less and less civilized. The number of pumps decrease. The style of pumps goes further and further back in time. The stations get farther and farther from the interstate. The employees get more rustic and less social as I press on. I used to make a habit out of stopping and eating one of those Mexican-style "Tornado" things that roll around on those food heaters at gas stations. Those are long gone. Now the pattern is to grab a water, a dusty bag of chips if I can, and roll on. I exit to fuel stops that have dirt roads, and as I pull in, a cloud of fine dust traces my path and remains in the air even after I have finished fueling. It's as if not even wind lives here anymore. The whole ride was becoming depressing. That does not fully capture it. It's more than that. The exits that finally interrupt the desolation and give you a small glimmer of hope that civilization exists still have that fucking stupid blue bottom rocker that reads "No Services", which adds a frosting of pissed-the-fuck-off to this depression cake. So, whatever the combination of pissed-the-fuck-off and depression results in is what this ride was turning into. The pattern seems to be nothing, and then more nothing, and then a stretch of nothing before you pull off for fuel, which turns into a series of streets filled with nothing, until you get to a pocket of civilization no bigger than the smallest suburb with a gas station in it. Then you reluctantly leave that little fistful of civilization and ride back into nothing.

These exits are starting to worry me, big time. So, instead of waiting until my low fuel light illuminates to warn me when to fuel like I started doing again, I start looking for fuel stops as soon as I clear around eighty miles again. The minute I see one, I hit it. The fucked-up thing about Utah that will drive you fucking nuts is the fact that there are some exits that have that now familiar sign that reads "No Services" and you're like, "Fuck!" and tear off. You go burning down the fucking road and when you look over, way out off the fucking interstate, there actually *is* a fuel station! What the fuck kind of shenanigans is that? Twice I had blown past an exit sign that said it had no services, when it did, and had to backpedal the motorcycle 200 feet on the breakdown lane back to the exit to get fuel. I should have just turned the bike around and rode in the opposite direction back to the fucking exit, but I took the opportunity to practice the useless skill of backpedaling a motorcycle in a straight line for hundreds of feet.

I am going to take a moment here to give a "Fuck you" in advance to Utah. See, I contemplated building this section of the story up with suspense and all that sexy shit. I was going to possibly run this part of the story down and keep you thinking that maybe Utah did not have some bullshit challenge in it, besides its annoyances that I already described. I was going to attempt to trick you by describing another storm that I battled through in Utah and make you think maybe that was going to be the big challenge Utah had for me. But I reconsidered. Utah, and the pussy-ass way that Utah played me, does not deserve those cute little writing tools. Utah can go back itself up against a doorknob and fuck itself. Now, to any readers from Utah who might feel some kind of way about my sentiments toward your stretch of state that borders I-70W: Well, in the year 2065, when Utah finally receives this crazy invention called the internet on one of those wacky gadgets called a laptop, and you realize I wrote these words when you go to digitally buy this book, I will personally give you a "Utah Discount" if you can prove you are from Utah. Then, I will also throw in a personally encapsulated, historical, vintage-edition FUCK YOU from the past. But wait, there's more: If you order now, I will throw in not one, but two FUCK YOUs so you can give one to the kiddos... Fuck Utah.

Now let me explain why the I feel this way. Apparently, Utah thinks it's a wise idea to have a stretch of interstate that does not have a fueling point on it for 106 miles! Supposedly (I heard this after the fact), there is a sign that warns you of this fucking ridiculousness. I did not see this fucking sign. I got an idea for you, Utah. Instead of having nine million fucking exit signs that say "No Services" under them, why don't you put how many fucking miles to the next fucking service area on them. That is the information we as motorists are looking for. (Just writing this part of the story is re-pissing me off!) I swear if any motorcyclist passes through this state after

105

reading this book, take a fucking can of spray paint with you, and do the right thing. Take care of the soldiers behind you. The shit is ridiculous.

I guess you wouldn't even notice if you are in a car and can eat miles like that up with no problem. Maybe you don't even care as much as I do if you have travelled this stretch of road and had a reserve tank of fuel, like I once did, in your saddlebags. You probably would pull that thing out like, "Wow, glad I brought this. Never thought I would actually use it." You would fuel up and travel on, never processing the calamity of your situation. Well good for you. That would be a nice boring little six sentences in *your* story. But, this is not *your* story. This is Hood, Outcast MC, and this is *my* fucking story. So, no, I don't have my extra two gallons of fuel to rescue me. No, I don't have saddlebags with the typical Gatorade bottle of fuel in it that is going to save my ass. I don't even have saddle-bags anymore! No, I don't have a group of "bros" with me that are going to eventually laugh at me over a drink because my "scoot" ran out of fuel in Utah. Fuck you! (Now reader, you might be one of those fuck-faced pricks that finds it as their duty to state obvious observations like, "Well, all that's your fault." Yeah, no shit, you foreskin! (In retrospect, much of this trip is an ode to my ignorance and it is showing me how much I don't know. But I don't realize that yet. In the moment I am upset.) But, I got this fucking far, under the same conditions, right? I traveled from Massachusetts, which borders the fucking Atlantic Ocean, and have traveled through a shitload of states and even fucked around with another country, and I made it, right? So, either all these other states are ironically governed by the same secret society that declares fuel stops should be within 106 miles of each other on an interstate, and Utah seceded from this sect, or Utah can go fuck itself! So, reader, if you are one of those people to comment like that then you probably are the type of person that sees things wrong in the world but has that pussy-ass attitude like, "Well, as long as it's not me then..." and turns a blind eye. I despise people like you and hope you get hit by a fucking yacht!

Ok, so obviously I am tooling around on this fucking stretch of highway, and I am pretty much close to seventy or eighty miles into my tank. I see a sign that says there is fuel at exit whatever-the-fuck. So, I ride to exit whatever-the-fuck, which is a few more miles out of the tank. I pull off of nothing into the middle of fucking nothing. No bullshit, the exit is just more road off the interstate that is surrounded by medium mountainous terrain and wild grass. That road then turns into a completely unmarked intersection with an empty open shack at the corner! What the fuck is this?! How the fuck am I supposed to... I don't even know what the name of this new road I'm on is! Nothing is marked! GPS and all that sexy shit is nonexistent in these wastelands. As in your GPS reads "searching for GPS signal". So, if I were to get lost, or had any other form of an issue, the deeper I go into this no man's land, the more fucked I am. I travel a good ten miles in a direction that brings me to another desolate intersection (I hope you're doing the math to my fuel consumption). Fuck that, I turn back and return to the first intersection with the shack. I go in the opposite direction of the way I first went for about five miles. I don't like it at all. It looks like a jigsaw of bullshit with nothing marked. Nope. Ok, if some exits can *not* have fuel signs, but they *do* have fuel stations, then it would not surprise me that there are exits in Utah that have signs for fuel with no fuel stations at them. My best bet is to get back on the main strip and try and *putt-putt* this bitch out to the next exit, and hopefully that shit has something... anything.

I'm somewhere close to 110 miles into my tank now. Typically my fuel light would have turned on by now, but it hasn't, so I'm getting a lot out of this tank (when the light turns on I have about another forty miles I can go). I slow to 40 mph and roll in the breakdown lane to try and

107

get the most out of my tank. It's not looking good. I see some dudes in a Camaro pulled over up ahead. It looks like they are taking pictures. I roll up to them and ask them do they know if there is fuel ahead? They say they just came from that direction and that there is a town called Whatever-The-Fuck that has fuel. I ask them how far is town Whatever-The-Fuck? They look at each other, twist up their lips and face, shrug and agree that it's about fifteen minutes up the way.

They jump back in their Camaro and peel off. I continue *putt-putting* at 40 mph watching my mileage increase from 115 to 120. I watch it turn to 128, then I see the fuel light come on. I keep trudging along. I am still surrounded by nothing! No one is on the fucking road. 128 turns into 132, when I see a green sign way off in the distance. I can probably make it to that sign. If I run out of fuel it will suck, because I will have to leave the bike then ruck march off the exit to wherever the fuel is. If there even is fuel at this fucking exit. Those two dudes say there was, but who knows. I plop along closer to the sign. It looks smaller than an exit sign, which is strange. I keep riding. It could just be that my eyes don't have anything else to reference its size to.

As I get closer I realize it *is* smaller than a road exit sign. It is not a road exit sign at all. It is a green sign that tells you the distances to the next three immediate towns. Whenever I have seen these signs in Utah it typically is where fuel is. These are those little fistfuls of civilization I was talking about earlier. The top one, which is the closest one, is the town those two dudes were talking about: Whatever-The-Fuck town is thirty-eight miles away! I'm already at 132. My tank got 146 miles in Massachusetts and has not been close to that since. Especially when I have been attacking. There is no way, period, that I am going to get 170 miles out of my tank. Even if I can squeeze another twenty miles out of my tank, which is highly unlikely, that would bring me to 152 miles, which would mean I would still have eighteen miles to get to the next exit. I'm thinking, *If I do have to ruck it out what am I working with?* That would be hours of marching, which is going to put me well into the night. See, having a bike that won't start or getting your heart broken because you lost all of your shit is one thing. But, when your physical safety is threatened, shit raises to a whole other level. I will literally be stranded during dusk, which turns to night in about four hours, in the middle of nowhere. I have on all black clothes and will be completely invisible. No one is going to pull over for me. Shit, I wouldn't even pull over for me.

The phone has no signal out here. I mean possibly, highly unlikely, one could march until a signal was available closer to that fistful of civilization. This shit just got severely real. There is absolutely no question I am about to be stranded and unable to contact anyone. There is no question that my environment is even less hopeful than my odds at making it to the next exit. There is only one inevitable outcome to this situation. I am fucked. After what happened in Colorado, I kind of accidentally allowed the possibility of not making it to California to penetrate my psyche. I realized it as a very realistic outcome. I just did not think it would be like this! This is not good. My tank is at 148 miles. This is the most I have gotten out of my tank to date, so I know this is it. It is settling in that I am severely fucked despite my iron horse giving everything she has and stretching this tank out further than she has stretched any tank before. It's only minutes, if even, before she starts to have that empty stall. I can't believe this shit. I am fucking angry, which is the least bothersome of my emotions. I am also annoyed and hungry. That is a pretty dangerous combination but is not as bothersome as my last noticeable emotion. I am worried, which is the precursor to being scared, which is the most dangerous combination I could have right now. Panic is the inevitable result of these emotions, if not controlled. A plan

109

is the only way to control that combination, and I do not have one.

I roll along waiting to feel or hear the stutter in her engine signaling her decline. I listened for it. I heard something. It is happening. I hear her engine struggling. I want to just stop because I almost don't want her to die for no reason. She sputters. I'm not going to be any better off. I hear her engine going into new tones as she struggles. It almost sounds like she is getting louder. It's as if she is calling out to me for help. I feel like I'm putting a dog down. Her engine gets slightly louder it seems? It's like my brain is really magnifying and absorbing her last words. She gave it her all. But, no, she gets a hair louder. I'm kind of confused by this. Is the bike dying for real? Is something wrong? Why is she getting louder? Wait a minute, that's not me. That sound is not us! I look over my shoulder and see one light blaring down the road behind me. Then I see another light, and three more lights. Fuck! I start waving my hand franticly and pointing at my tank! Coming up behind me is the pack of touring bikes I rode with briefly in Colorado. They pull up next to me. I scream out, "I'm not going to make it!" The first biker signals to me to pull over. My horse stuttered and died right then, but no one noticed except me. She still had her pride. She was still standing. I was more than proud of her.

The pack surrounded me. They were men in their early fifties to early sixties of various descent. Their spirits were happy and harmless. We all understood what the situation was. I asked if any of them had a fuel canister. None of them had a fuel canister with fuel in it. How are they going to help me then? We start, kind of, standing around and pointing out silly details like, "Hey Mike, how big is your tank?" "I don't know about six something." One of them breaks through the huddle with a package in his hands and says, "I wasn't even going to bring this thing. Then I thought, 'why not?'" He laughs. We all look down and some let out vocal noises as we recognize and read the package. It's a siphoning kit. We rip the package open. No one has used one of these before. As one reads, the rest of us are trying to figure this thing out. They are comical with it. Corny, light-hearted jokes accompany the endeavor. "I think your tank has to be lower than his tank," one of them declares. We blindly agree. So, I move my bike lower on the slope off of the road. The supplying bike now has to be moved next to my bike. We are fussing around with this thing, and pumping it, which is applying suction, but nothing is happening. Then someone says, "I have an idea. Why don't you use this?" Instead of going from one bike to the other, we decided to attempt extracting from one bike into an emptied soda bottle placed on the ground. We are pumping the actuator and doing all the nonsense we were doing before. Then fuel began to rush through the clear tube and fill the soda bottle. Yup, the thing worked! I filled one bottle, then another. The man on the supplying bike suggested I take a third bottle, which I did. I was rescued. It was such a strange feeling.

We all suited back up, together. I felt like I had my pack with me. We all revved up and moved out. I start throwing up Outcast hand signals out of habit, then realized I was doing it and stopped. These dudes have no idea what that stuff is. They are not a Social Club, or Riding Club, or Traditional MC, or a 1%er organization. They are just men on motorcycles enjoying a ride, and they just rescued me and became my pack. The only pack I have had this whole trip. They did not roll in a tight, neat formation like Outcast. They did not have disciplined road maneuvers like Outcast. They rode along with their DOT regulation helmets, at their own slow speed, with their unregulated spacing. They took as much or as little space as they needed. They did not wear any cuts or vests. They wore whatever randomly colored riding suit they wanted to. I was the outlaw in the pack, but they are the ones that did not follow any rules. Interesting. I broke off from the pack with a bunch of waving, thumbs up, and other greetings

111

that were not middle fingers, to fuel up. Minutes later they pulled in to fuel up too. From this point on, every fuel stop in Utah I stopped at, no matter how little fuel I used. Fuck Utah!

I don't know at what point I was finally out of Utah because it was nighttime now, and I could not see mile markers. I know I saw signs for Las Vegas, while in Utah, so I knew the next state was going to be Nevada, but I couldn't tell you at what point I crossed into Nevada. I have been riding for hours. The fuel stops were respectfully spaced. The temperature was decent. The weather was mild. I did not see or smell a rain cloud anywhere. I didn't see much of anything. The road was completely void of light. I must be in Nevada. Honestly, I didn't really care at this point. I was drained. I cleared a lot of states, and a piece of my enthusiasm was left in each one. As I rode through the desert I felt numb. I would roll into a fuel station, fuel the bike, drink a Red Bull, and ride out. The Red Bulls were not having an effect anymore. They were not giving me any perceivable energy at this point. They were just giving me flashbacks.

The first time I ever had Red Bull, and the most I ever drank Red Bull, was in Iraq during my first deployment. I had never tasted this beverage before in my life and then, somehow, due to whatever angles were worked out, we had pallets of this shit in the middle of the desert. We might have had more cases of Red Bull than we had water. That's how much we had. It had to have been a loophole or some kind of decision made by our command, because it was not typical. So, needless to say, I drank copious amounts of Red Bull in Iraq. Which is insane if you think about it. To this day, whenever I drink a Red Bull, it immediately gives me a sensation of being in Iraq. My brain forever associates the taste of that beverage with certain scenes I specifically can recall from Ashraf.

112

(Certain operations in Ashraf were a secret then but can be found online now.)

So, in Nevada, as I rode with the flavor of Red Bull on my tongue through the night, I would drift off into different memories I have about some of my experiences in Iraq. Not the heart-racing, high adrenaline kinetic stuff, but more so some of the scents and the visuals I had. During my second tour, I would think about pulling up to the edge of the Tigris River and staring into it. I recall being at the Euphrates River as well. I remember the feeling of the sun and how all the trees around the rivers made a jungle environment as opposed to all the desert with which I had grown so familiar. I would think how I was familiar with these rivers from The Bible, but to stand over them felt significant. It felt spiritual. Iraq is one of the most amazing places I have ever been in my life and to explore it to the degree I did during my second tour, despite all the warfare, was an honor.

As I rode along this dark road in the deserts of Nevada, appreciating my experiences in the deserts of Iraq, I came across an awesome sight. I rolled gradually over a hill, and there in front of me in the middle of the blackness, was a city full of lights. The place was electric. It was a Mecca of yellow lights and flashing signs. The city was still miles away, but I was riding towards it. It was like nothing I have ever seen before. It literally interrupts the blackness. There is no gradual progression. It goes from blackness to a city of lights, just like that.

Eventually my motorcycle covered the miles of highway from the top of that hill and is cutting into this sea of lights. Surprisingly, I am immediately resistive; I'm unsure why. But, I hit one city of lights and flashing moving signs. It was an overwhelming swarm of flashing, casino-related signs. It's too much. If everything is trying to get your attention, ultimately, nothing gets your attention. I kept riding hoping to see something that would

113

change my resistiveness, but I didn't. At last, that city turned into darkness again. A couple of fuel stops later, another city of lights interrupts the darkness. This one is just a little heavier than the last one but the same lame approach. It seems exhausted and tired. I was not impressed. I floated through that city, and it also turned to blackness again. A tank of fuel later another city of lights, even bigger than the other two, showed its face. If they all are not considered Las Vegas, then *this* has to be Las Vegas. The whole fucking city is a light show! I don't recall paying attention to any highway signs. Again, when everything is trying to grab your attention, nothing gets it.

I pull off of the highway and decide I'm going to get a taste of this city. I am going to recharge and replenish. I'll stay the night in a hotel, absorb the energy of Las Vegas, and then head out sometime when the sun is up. I start asking around for a hotel, and I get directed to some place. The hotel is a huge Casino. Everything is a fucking casino. It's ridiculous. There are slot machines in fucking gas stations! I'm surprised when you go to the restroom the fucking toilet paper doesn't have a bunch of 7s on it. The shit is cheesy. I still don't know why, but I'm completely not enjoying any of this shit. I go to the hotel/casino lobby. I go to ask for information at a desk mobbed by people. There are a ton of people behind me. I realize that I have just cut a line of people that folds over about five times. They are zombies with fake, plastered smiles on their faces acting like they are dazzled by this bullshit. They are dressed the way people dress when they go on vacation that just screams that they're tourists. I watch the local employees (that all appear to be Native American or Mexican) who are looking unenthused. They weave in and around the zombie-tourists, cleaning silently, picking up plastic cups filled with ice and the remnants of watered down alcohol. They look exhausted. Everything looks exhausted. The City that Never Sleeps needs a nap. It needs one more than I do. Fuck this place. I about-face and march

114

out the door to my motorcycle. We are moving on. I'm not saying that I will not crash somewhere for the night, but I am saying I'm not crashing here. There's too much hoopla and fuckery going on around me. There's too much forced happiness and forced drinking. It all feels false and forced. I don't like the energy. It's distracting in an unsettling way. It has been years since I have been in settings this active. After I returned from Afghanistan, that was pretty much a thing of the past. I'm not a fan of it. I leave.

The three cities of lights slowly become histories that barely are remembered after I have left them. Nevada starts to normalize again. I keep riding. Now, *I* am starting to feel like a zombie. It is deep into the nighttime. I have been up since 0645 hrs. It's late. I'm tired, and I need fuel. My GPS has drained my cell phone battery down to nothing even while plugged to the power source. Everything I own is exhausted. I hit a burger joint. It's too late to go in so only the drive-thru is open. Using the drive-thru on a motorcycle is annoying. I eat in the parking lot real quick. I go to fuel up, and my phone dies. No phone means no GPS. It's time to charge everything including myself. I pull out the duster, move the bike on the sidewalk in front of a bench, and commence power charging everything. I plug the phone into the outdoor wall socket next to the bench, rest my weapon against my chest, and power nap in my duster. Maybe a half hour later, I get up from the bench, attach my phone to the OAC, mount up, and gun it out of there. I'm way too close to Los Angeles to stop now. I need this mission to be over. I need victory.

So, instead of seeking a place to regroup, I decide we are power-pushing into California and closing this out tonight. I think I'm too tired to fully commit to attack posture. I don't feel like Night Wolf, and I don't feel like Hood. I don't feel. I just am moving now. I'm just bringing it all in. My rucksack feels like a burden. My boots feel heavy. My gloves feel restrictive. My subconscious DJ

115

scrambles to try and throw the Bon Jovi record on, "Sometimes I sleep, sometimes it's not for days, and the people I meet always go their separate ways..." I don't want to remember hearing anything. I don't want to think about anything. I just want to get to this clubhouse and crack a beer. I'm spent.

(X-Ray, this is Night Wolf, RP Outcast Base one pack, one victor, time 0400 hrs, end of mission how copy? over) I rumbled slowly past the clubhouse, unsure if this was actually the place, then circled back around and pulled down the side-street when the big, black gate that secured the clubhouse began to slide open. The mission was to arrive in Los Angeles, California at the Clubhouse on Saturday, no later than 11:00 AM. It was 4:00 AM on that date. The last leg, which started in Colorado from that motel, to here was a little over 1,100 miles in one day. But, I was here. I made it. I just traveled by myself from a state bordering the Atlantic Ocean to one bordering the Pacific Ocean on my iron. It was Patches opening the gate for me, exposing all the parked motorcycles inside. I rumbled slowly into the gate. "I just heard you, man. So, I came out," he says. "Park right there." I am stumbling and misjudging the cut necessary to back the bike smoothly into the space. It's a simple parking maneuver but I'm all fucked up doing it. Patches is watching me kind of like, *what the fuck?* He volunteers to park the bike for me, but I manage to stumble the shit in there. I think moving forward at high speed for as long as I have been today then having to use my legs was a task my body was not equipped to handle at this level of fatigue. Again, however, I got it done. I got off my motorcycle. I looked at her and put my hand on her tank. "Good job," I say.

Patches tells me everyone is sleeping in the clubhouse so no sense in going in. He suggests I go to the hotel that is about a one-minute walk down the street where the rest of the Massachusetts bros are. The fact that I am here is overwhelming! I'm overwhelming Patches a little. I feel like I'm screaming when I talk, 'cause riding with the wind and pipes has made my ears feel like I came out of a nightclub. We walk to the hotel room where Three Piece is. I walk in and see him crack that signature, Three Piece, half-smile smirk while shaking his head slowly. "I made it, motherfucker!" I declare. He looks me up and down, "How was it?" I start to answer, "Man, listen…" I don't even know where to begin. I decide that it's too much for me to even tell right now. He continues the conversation for me with questions to the portions of the story he knows, "Why didn't you go home when you lost all your shit?" He looks genuinely confused. "He's stubborn!" is the sentence Patches interjects with.

Seeing my bros has gotten me fired up now, so I'm pacing back and forth and placing my gear down in odd places then picking it up and putting it in a different place. I have not seen another vest with an Old Man on it in a long time so I'm excited, and I can't stop the energy. "Fuck that. What the fuck is the difference between me pushing forward and pushing backward? I still don't have my shit!" I answer. Three Piece looks at me silently with that smirk and just shakes his head again. He looks at Patches and says, "I knew he wasn't going to stop. I said, 'He's gonna keep coming, and coming, and coming.'" He shakes his head some more then turns away. I continue moving my gloves from here to there. Placing my goggles down then picking them up and putting them away. I have no clue what I'm doing. I can't believe I just rode across the motherfucking country! I took a fucking shortcut through another country! What the fuck! Ha! Wow! Yeah, I'm fired up. All that fatigue seems to have completely left me, or is the cause of this euphoric state I'm in. Three Piece extends his hand with an envelope in it! "Here." They explain to me what the money is for. I count it. I love this Outcast shit. I take off my duster, my leather coat, my leather scarf and reach into my rucksack. Sound is vacuumed from the room for a moment. When my hands come out Three Piece and Patches both fall to the ground, grabbing their ears to protect them from the loud harmony of naked black angels with black wings singing out from their guts a soulful cry of pleasure. (I'm telling you, this is exactly how it happened!) I hold the vest, with The Old Man on it, up in the air. The Old Man laughs out loud. It's a hearty, raspy, proud laugh. It's a decrepit laugh. It's an all-black-everything, middle-fingers-up, ride-for-a-piece-of-everything laugh. It's an Outcast laugh.

Day Six

I grab a few hours of sleep. Patches and Three Piece are restless. Patches is in and out, just kind of doing what Patches does. A little about Patches: He's a seasoned biker. He's an old school brother that ends almost all his sentences with an accentuated, 80's-style "yuh know". He's the Sergeant at Arms of our chapter. Patches is an interesting dude. He definitely walks to the beat of his own drum. He's Outcast for sure. Three Piece gets up out of the bed still disgruntled about something. He is explaining either to Patches or re-confirming to himself how he is not riding with anyone back. He explains to me how his journey coming out here sucked. He gives recognition to the challenges I had by saying, "I mean it wasn't like your shit..." before he continues with, "The dude dropped his bike twelve times!" Now, Patches chimes in and confirms what Three Piece just said, "Twelve times, man." I ask, "Who dropped their shit twelve times?" Three Piece gets even more animated as he responds, "The fuckin' old dude. Fuckin, uh, fucking Choppa!" He goes into explaining how when they rolled to New Jersey, which was their first stop from Massachusetts, they picked up Choppa. He is a much older, and worn-down, bro from Ohio. This must have been his last significant ride, Three explains. According to Three, he made the journey miserable. He rode slowly, making it difficult to keep the pack together. He made potentially dangerous riding scenarios. Patches would occasionally pop in the conversation confirming everything Three Piece was saying. Three shook his head, "It was a fucking set up! They passed him off to us. I'm not rolling back with that dude." I went into my spiel to Three, "Bro, he's old! We all going to get there. At some point you, me, we all going to be that dude. You did the right thing, you

119

can't leave the dude." I'm laughing. Three Piece is not. "Then you can roll back with him. I'm not rolling back with him. That shit was a setup," he says. Patches starts two-stepping, which he does when he gets all into what he is saying. He adds his piece to the story, "The worst was when we rolled to the gas station, man. I got the pack all tight and pretty and shit. Everyone is in formation. The shit looked good, yuh know! Some white boys roll up on their shit." He adjusts his glasses before he continues. "I'm about to pull the formation in front of them. Show them how Outcasts do, yuh know. He drops his shit right there, man! I mean, he went down flat. They all come running to help him. The shit was embarrassing, man." He's kind of laughing. "He don't even try to save himself. That's how many times he dropped his shit. He don't even try and save himself. He just tucks and rolls like 'whoop', yuh know!" I'm laughing. I say again, "Leave no man behind."

I rested a little bit in the hotel, but it's pointless to try and sleep now. There are no extra washcloths or towels in the room, but I see an employee with the towel cart in the parking lot. I run up on him and come back with a bunch of washcloths and towels for the bros. I shower up and suit up. I don't see Three Piece anymore or Patches. I text Three to see where he is. I'm not too concerned though. I'm by myself again. I obviously have no problem with that. I take off to the clubhouse to go meet my California bros.

This hood feels familiar even though I have never been here before. I stroll down the street past the convenience store. The type of store that has the pay phone outside with paint-pen graffiti and rap group promotional stickers all over it. It has a rack of pork rinds next to the teller's booth, which is encased in plexiglass. They sell the same shit in every hood convenience store. You get Goya beans, rolling papers, a beef patty, weed baggies, cheese curls, a champagne soda, and scratch tickets in one swoop at the hood convenience store. A forty-five second walk in one direction is a liquor store. A one-minute walk in the other direction is another liquor store and a fish shop. The check cashing shack is diagonally across the street. I absorb this neighborhood. The hood can remind you of poverty and depress you if you let it. Or, its familiarity can make you real comfortable. I'm real comfortable right now, and I am in real good spirits. A group of old timers are next to a house near a dilapidated Cadillac. The scene is also familiar. I swear in every hood is an old Cadi that some old dude won't let go of. It probably has memories of when he felt best about himself, or when he had youthful fun. If you ever get to speak to the owner, he will tell you how there is no better car than a Cadillac. He will also tell you how this one is good; she just needs (insert any car part you want). The car usually becomes a half-tarped, landmark that blocks a space in the driveway. It's all so familiar. They nod to me, and I nod to them.

The clubhouse is right there, but I decide to walk around the hood for a little bit. I walk past some place of worship that looks like someone's apartment. I walk to the fish store next to the liquor store. I order a fishplate from the store. I have no idea why but The Old Man on my back must like fried fish, because it seems that every time I have my rags on in another state, I end up eating fried fish with beer. I grab two tall cans of Colt 45 and crack one open outside while I wait for my fish plate to cook. I call my wife while I'm outside. I'm a simple dude, and I'm happy right now. It's little things, like my Colt 45, and the anticipation of my fish plate, that are making me happy in this moment. I'm happy to pace back and forth outside in the energy of this neighborhood, on my phone, only interrupted to occasionally throw a head nod to people entering the store. I'm good in the hood. I always am. I talk to my ol' lady, and it all feels familiar: me neck deep in some random state, or random tarmac, or random training base, walking around in an aimless circle, talking to my

121

wife. It's been so many years of this pattern existing, but I barely even realized it. Like I said before, I didn't communicate with anyone in boot camp, except the one or two letters that were exchanged between her and me.

It was at boot camp that I first got exposed to the life-long army term of "battle buddy". Basically, it was the dude whose last name was closest alphabetically to yours who now became your fucking hip. He was on the top bunk and you were on the bottom. You were assigned to each other as brothers, and Lord help you if you were found anywhere, doing anything, without your battle buddy. "Private So-and-So, where the hell is your doggone battle buddy?!" would be heard from some drill sergeant flying out of some corner. If you got smoked (physical correction to the point of exhaustion) for some shit you did wrong, your battle buddy got smoked with you. Many times, unaware of why he was even being smoked. Over time, the entire platoon becomes your battle buddy. You call everyone in your group "Battle". "Aye, Battle, grab the end of this and lift on three." It becomes a term of unity, that started with that connection, between you and that person assigned to you.

My ol' lady has been my battle buddy for a while. We have been through a lot. She is the silent partner in all of this. Like a battle buddy, I feel responsible for her, and her me. It's one thing when you are with someone through good times and bad times and all, but when you feel responsible for someone it's a whole other dynamic to the relationship. No matter what your outcome is, you make sure that person is ok. It has a sense of duty to it. It's not questioned or spoken of. It is just done. Anyway, my food plate is ready, my first beer is finished, and my conversation with my battle buddy has done whatever intangible thing that it does that makes us both feel complete. It's not something expressed. It's something you just hear. I can hear when she's solid. I hang up and walk my fish plate and my other beer back to the clubhouse.

I walk through the open gate. Blacked out bikes are everywhere. I walk past a Harley with damn near half the engine taken apart. It's right next to my horse, which looks fucking insane. I never really got an opportunity to look at her much, because I have been riding her. Maybe it's because I have not seen her next to another vehicle while on this trip until now, but she looked like she just came back from war! The other bikes are generally shiny and decent, but my bike is a different story. The windshield and headlight are completely covered with dead bugs. Her front end is layered with dust that has turned into caked-on mud. I sprayed parts of her with black paint and Plasti-Dip back home. The paint was gradually ripped off as if the bike rolled through a shower of gravel. The Plasti-Dip had peeled and released off in patches. She didn't look bad, she just looked like she... I don't know. Like she rode across the nation! I was proud of it. That was undeniable proof that this bike and its rider have been pounding pavement. I see lower rockers from everywhere. I greet bro after bro, "What up? Hood, Massachusetts." They greet me back, "Jazz Black, Arizona. How you doing brother? Did you say Massachusetts?" Jazz has that voice that directly correlates to his name. He carries a pleasant attitude, like he has been around the world twice and has a story for every city you can name. He sounds like he smoked a pack of cigarettes for every one of those stories since he was, like, eight. "That's what I like to see, man! Young brothers riding their shit!" Our conversation started with that sentiment. Then we just go into it with laughter and jokes and handshakes. "Have you met..." Jazz starts introducing me to more bros. I meet Beast and Raw from Illinois. The stories continue. More laughter ensues. I kill my fishplate with other bros who can't refuse my offer. I meet Tone, from California. We look at each other like we have met before. We start talking. Tone's a cool-ass dude. He might have been twisting it up as we talked. Then he floated away probably to smoke it.

I have not even made it inside yet, and I have already started forgetting names of all the bros I'm meeting. Eventually, I make it inside the clubhouse and, *wow*! California's clubhouse is pretty fucking impressive to me. It still has that gritty Outcast flavor to it, but it's one of the sexier clubhouses I have seen so far. Mirrors are all over that bitch. I see the stage that is just big enough for a strip pole, even though one is not there, in between the pool table area and the bar area. I'm sure it's in some back room somewhere. The clubhouse has everything you need: A garage in the back, plus a parking area, a hotel in walking distance, the security gate, a barbecue area with a tent and seating, a pool table area, seats and tables, couches, a serious horseshoe shaped bar, a full kitchen behind the bar, and several bathrooms. They are doing ok in California, it seems. The handshakes and name exchanges don't stop. If I don't know a bro, I introduce myself. Somebody screams out, "See, that's the shit I'm talking about. That's good. 'Cause, you know, you got these bros that will be there the whole night and never move off their stool to talk to anyone." The bros at the bar resound in moans of agreement. It starts a small conversation about how bros have to meet each other and communicate. I continue talking with each bro and listening to them. It got to the point where I would walk up to bros and introduce myself, and they would laugh because we already met outside. "That's right. That's right. Big Worm, North Carolina." What can I say, Outcast has a lot of bros. I meet POs like Shelly and Lady Evil. I converse with them, which ultimately results in me meeting their sponsors.

I can't readily identify what bro is working the bar, so I announce that I am walking behind the bar to get my reward beer! I target lock on a suspicious looking white cooler oddly placed over there. Bingo, it's a cache of cold ones. I grab a Heineken and exfiltrate the kitchen. I tear the cap off with my teeth and toast to myself. I made it. There is a whole spread of food the POs cooked inside and food being barbecued outside. I go back outside with a beer and more bros are rolling in. I take a seat while speaking with various bros and continue watching bros roll in. They all have their machines that are reflections of their characters. They all have their different Outcast styles.

One bro rolls in on his machine and scans for a place to put it. He doesn't see one so he powers down his iron in the center of the parking lot. He takes his time removing his mask. I think to let everyone absorb it, but it adds dramatic tension to his presentation. His mask is the same restraint that was used on Hannibal Lecter. I have seen various skull masks, but I have never seen that before. He takes it off. He walks right to me even though I have not seen him before. He speaks in a slow, well-enunciated manner, "What's up bro. Solo. California." He pounds my hand and hugs me. "What up, bro. Hood, Massachusetts." We start talking. It's really something else when you meet so many bros at once because some of them, for no readily understandable reason, you just bond with immediately. It makes you bird's-eye the situation and try to extract some type of pattern. Solo and I bonded like that. Nothing crazy, it wasn't like we were besties, or like I wanted him to marry my sister and shit. But, he stood out to me, and I stood out to him. So, we continually kicked it throughout my time in California. That's my dude.

There was a power-run being orchestrated. Patches was scrambling around trying to get that all situated. I asked Three Piece if he was rolling. He said he already has done all this shit, so he was not rolling. Three eventually disappeared for good that day. Patches rolled on the power-run, which was short, and I continued networking with Cast. This club has some fucking characters in it. I say that, to say this: Those fucking Arizona boys are some motherfucking funny-ass good dudes! These dudes, every

125

single one of them, had me split open the minute we met. Bitch Tamer (yeah, that's his name!), Dark Vader, and the bro with the mohawk, JMo. I don't know what the fuck is in the water in Arizona, but those motherfuckers are all fucking marbleless. I think I liked everyone who was from that chapter immediately. They made me promise to stop through on my way back to Boston. I had no idea what the path was going to be on my way back. I was going to be with a pack this time so, if not this time, I was going to be in Arizona at some point. Patches and the rest of the group that rolled out on the power-run return.

The presidents meeting is about to take place. Patches rolls in to represent Massachusetts. Three Piece re-appears and is surprised the meeting started already. I see bros tinkering with the Harley that is next to mine. We start talking lightly. I see an old man I recognize. He stayed in the hotel room I was in when I was a probie one time at the mother chapter. "Hood, Massachusetts," I say. The brother looks battered and weakened. He looks like he has been hitting the bottle since Martin had a dream. His nose has been sunburned and the dark layer of burnt skin has started to separate off his face and reveal the light pink layer of fresh skin underneath. He looks concerned as he watches them tinker with the bike. His concentration was interrupted by my greeting. He involuntarily lights up and responds with a hug. He mumbles something, *Mumble, mumble, mumble* "...Choppa!" *mumble, mumble*. Well shit, it's Three Piece's boy! I smile as all the stories of him dropping the bike flash in my head. "How was your trip?" I ask. He responds, *Mumble, mumble, mumble* "...this motherfucker!" he exclaims as he points with two hands to the disassembled Harley then grabs his head and continues, *Mumble, mumble, mumble* "...so I can get home!"

I start talking to the bros near the Harley. I ask what the symptoms were to the bike going down. That question turns to this question, then wrenches start coming out, and screwdrivers, and before I know it I'm neck deep

126

into the engine with a few other bros. I'm a full-time diesel mechanic as a civilian job so maintenance theory is not far from my lane at all. I absolutely have no zeal for it, but working on motorcycles has some sort of appeal to me. I enjoy doing all the work on my machine. It's pretty much the only part of maintenance I still enjoy. I don't mind fixing trucks, but it's just work to me. Motorcycles, I actually enjoy although I don't know too much. I want the machine to come back alive. I want the horse to run! We are going in on this bike.

A bro walks through the gate and is scanning all the bikes. He says, "Who's iron is this?" while staring at my horse. I look over at him while other bros point me out. "That's Hood's shit, man. He came from Massachusetts on that." He stares, nods in respect of the information he just heard, then throws in, "Too bad it's not a Harley." From what I have seen, my bike is the only bike out of every bike on the premises that is not an American-made motorcycle. I know where the Harley connection comes from. I know the traditions of OMCs as well. At the time, our club allowed cruisers that were not American as long as the member didn't hold certain positions. So I was in good standing. I am used to the jovial, ball-busting that comes with having a non-American-made bike. I fire back, "Oh, you mean like this shit here!" As I point at the Harley Davidson I'm helping fix. Bros erupt in laughter. The battle is on now. Harley Davidson reinforcements come out of the woodwork and the prior owners of "Jap Bikes" fire shots in my defense. I continue, "She's here, from the other side of the country. What the fuck more do I have to say? How much was your Harley, bro... twenty, thirty? You know how much my bitch was?" I don't even give him a chance to process the question. I'm all fired up now. It's all in fun though, "$2,600! For $2,600, she outperforms and outlasts yours!" Bros are firing back and forth in the conversation, which is decorated with cursing and laughter.

127

HOOD LODO

I admire the traditional aspects of my club. It has been around since the late sixties. Pretty much all of the 1%er organizations have histories dating that far back and follow traditions founded by soldiers returning from war most likely isolated and seeking unity amongst each other on Harley Davidsons. The post-traumatic stress and its symptoms were probably self-remedied. Welcome to the birth of the traditional motorcycle club. I don't think I could align more than I already do with this history. It pretty much lines up exactly, except the Harley Davidson. Some bros come up to me and admit that their favorite bike was a Jap-bike. It's all love. I'm just feeling extremely protective over my bitch right now. I'm very proud of her, and I feel connected to the damn machine for real. I'm still on a high from arriving here this morning. I'm not hearing anyone talking shit about my bitch. The conversation ends with the bro giving me respect for my journey here. The shit talking is something that just comes with it all. We are Outcast. We give each other a middle finger to say "What's up". We say "Fuck you" to each other as a goodbye. It is what it is. When you are able to understand someone's intent, it doesn't really matter what their words are too much. Communication is more than words.

Three Piece slides up to me and speaks in my ear, "See, you going to start working on that bike. You probably going to get the thing running, and then you going to have to ride with him. I'm warning you." Choppa traumatized this dude! The shit must really have been a headache. Three Piece is the type of dude that might talk shit and all, but he would never leave that dude behind on the road. He might shake him here in California, but he would reliably bring him in from the road. Three Piece is going to probably shake *me* in California. I can already see how he's moving. He is smiling, but he is seriously straying away from anything that even looks like it could slow his progress back home. I think him hearing about all my challenges has him grouping me in the hazard bracket.

128

Minutes later he would stroll by again, see us hard at work on the Harley, look at me, shake his head and say, "I'm warning you."

The Harley was leaking oil and pissing out smoke from the engine. The push rods had backed out or something like that. Choppa had bought a gasket kit and all, but the solution was the push rods if I remember. I had nothing to do with the solution, so I don't honestly know. My focus was elsewhere. I had put my iron on the trickle charger, because I heard the dull clicks again that morning. The trickle charger showed a solid green light saying she was fully charged, but I was still getting that clicking sound. I'm laughing, hoping that the bro I just went to war with over this bike, saying how reliable she is, doesn't see this shit. A couple of other bros heard it and in unison told me I need a new battery. They told me an Auto Zone was down the street.

Sky Blue loads me up in his cage (cage is the term used for a car), and we go get that. Sky Blue is a pillar in this California camp. He's a solid dude. We get the battery, and now I'm pulling the seat off my bike while they are re-assembling the Harley next to me. It looks like an Outcast Motorcycle Repair shop outside. POs are seated behind us, drinking and watching what we are doing. I install the battery and re-attach my SAE power source. I turn the key and hear the fuel pump give a strong spray of fuel. I ignite her, and she rumbles instantly to life. Her headlight blares on a second later. Turmoil (one of bros who was fixing Choppa's bike) and I are talking about the tail-light. He works for Suzuki so he shows me exactly what to do and buy. I ride out to Auto Zone again. When I return, I park on the street, and I'm on my back under the ass of my bike with a beer one of the POs got me, fixing the light. We thought it was the lightbulb, but as I look closer the ground cable to the light socket had snapped off. Ok, back to Auto Zone for a light housing. I come back and install the housing, splice the wires and create a new connection. I test her out, and we are good. I grey tape all that shit off and go grab another beer.

I'm feeling good as shit. I ate good food inside earlier. I have had plenty of beer and a few shots with bros. Now, Sky Blue is playing some classic 90's music from the west coast back during the west-coast's glory days. I'm enjoying everything. We start talking about west coast music and artists. Somewhere in the conversation I talk about the song by Ice Cube called Friday (the one him and B Real of Cypress Hill ended up getting into conflict over) and how I liked the beat so much I had recorded the song off the movie while the movie was playing. Sky Blue laughed and told me I should have just hit him, and he would have had Ice Cube personally send the shit to me. A couple of brews later I'm by the pool table watching the bros play. In the corner, another bro has the clippers out and he has a line of bros ready to get their hair cut.

I get pulled outside and am talking to some bro who is like, "I can tell already just how you are; you gon' be a Victory man." I guess he heard my spiel during the Harley debate. He points proudly at a Victory, American-made, motorcycle across the street, and the shit is sexy. I go check it out. Shit, maybe he is right, but I plan on being on my bitch for a while, so no matter (little did either of us know how wrong we both were. Harley VROD Muscle all day).

I see Patches outside talking to a PO and her sponsor. I shake hands with Boogie, the National President at the time. Patches sees Boogie and walks with me back over to him, "You met Hood? He just rode his shit from Massachusetts, yuh know!" Boogie reaches in his pocket and pulls out a Cross Country Club patch. He signals to another bro and that bro reaches in his pocket and produces the California state patch for me. Patch or no patch, this is a motorcycle club, and it is a lifestyle. I would imagine that a cross-country journey is in every true biker's plan. Patches has made the trip, and although his name is patches, he chooses not to wear that patch. He doesn't wear his mother patch either. I respect that. It reminds me of the military. There are points you grow to and experiences you have that make the jewelry you wear on your chest unimportant to show. It's not about that. It does not remove from the sense of pride you have when you earned them, but you don't earn them to show off. Sometimes, I don't wear some of my combat patches. Sometimes I don't wear my badges and skill identifiers. I think the whole mind frame comes from experience and just realizing there's something more significant than these things. Sometimes the meaning has been tainted because you see soldiers badge chase, or you see officers put each other in for combat action badges who were not involved in combat. You observe the standards start to morph in order to allow certain people to "earn" the medals. It all makes it less necessary to display them when they have been disgraced by actions like that. (At this point, I don't yet know exactly how similar the motorcycle set is when it comes to shit like this). I am very proud right now with these two items in my vest pocket.

The sun has set, and nighttime is on our ass. I see two probies working. Outcast makes probies earn it. They have no idea how long their probationary period is, because it is undetermined. You will probie until you are sufficiently seen as Outcast material. It's an important phase in the brotherhood, because once you are an Outcast you can never be anything else. Even if you somehow lose your rags and are ousted from the nation, you cannot resurface somewhere else within the motorcycle community with some other rags on (at least that's how it's supposed to go). There is no respawn once you're dead to the nation. That's just outlaw protocol. I'm sure in every club there are situations and exceptions but that's the standard. As a probie, you have no idea what you're getting into. It's like being a private in the military trying to make

131

it through boot camp. You think you know what you are joining. You will learn a lot, but you never really know what the fuck all this shit is until it's too late, and you have crossed over. Even then, the journey is just beginning. You will never understand the military unless you are in that motherfucker for a long time. I don't care how many family members you have in it. I don't care how much you studied, read, and tried out for military-related shit. You will never truly grasp it until you do years in it. Likewise, Outcast MC is a world that you do not understand until you crack that hatch open and jump into the darkness. That's just the beginning.

I'm still green to all of this, and I like that. It actually feels good to be green at something again. I like having that blind pride and being loyal to my choice. I enjoy the freedom of ignorance. I enjoy the guiltlessness for as long as I can, because I know it does not last forever. I speak with the probies temporarily and probe them for where they are in their journey. I extract what they know so far about the choice they are making. I challenge them with a few of the key points of information they need to know. I want a probie to win if that probie displays quality clay and can be molded like that. I isolate one probie, because he is giving me those type of cocky, open-ended answers that make me ask him more questions. I have been there. He will learn over time how to be a smart probie. I teach him with discipline, dismiss the probie, and continue on my path.

A bunch of bros are mobilizing to go to a party that is going on at Mi Palazio in Los Angeles. I will eventually roll. I am still socializing with the bros that are staying back at the clubhouse. I notice my name is the biggest name on the wall of the clubhouse. I blazed it earlier in chalk. I don't mean to do that, but I just realized that the type of way I write my name takes that space. I sign it the same way in each clubhouse. The only clubhouse I have been to in which my name is not blazed on the wall is my own in Massachusetts. I could force that to have some sort of significance, but it doesn't. I just have not done it yet. It's like tattooing your name on yourself to me. I bang back a few shots. Let me hit this fucking party up. At first, I wasn't going to go because I just don't do parties much anymore, but I'm out here and don't want to squander the experience.

I mount up on my iron. I have my Florida Outcast soft colors on. I don't recall who I got this shirt from. One of my bros gave it to me when I crossed over. I punch the address into my GPS, slap my goggles down, strap my helmet on and burn out to Los Angeles. I get to the event, and there are a lot of bikes outside. Probies are directing me where to park. I choose to park in the beginning of all the bikes where the street begins. The whole street is laced with bikers. I hear, "Hood!" on a side street. I walk up to the parked vehicle. A pair of my bros is standing on the passenger side of the vehicle talking on the sidewalk. A bro points to a bottle on the passenger seat floor and invites me to a swig. I do, then he does, and we talk for a bit. A female is in the car, but I don't think she is a PO. She might have been fixing her makeup, rolling a blunt, or loading a gun. I wasn't paying too much attention to her. Well, I was. But, I just don't remember everything about this party, 'cause I have been drinking all damn day.

With that being said, I'm going to jump a bunch of hours later into the night to the only real significant thing that happened. I'm outside by the bikes. There are a shitload of Cast everywhere, but we are not the only organization out here. We have some of our support clubs with us too like Black Kings. I like seeing clubs with Outcast support patches on. One Black King, who met me earlier at the clubhouse, came up to me and slapped hands with me. I tell him again how I dig what the Kings are doing a lot; he is nodding and running down to me what their plans are and how he would like to see chapters in in

133

all the states Cast has chapters. When he names Boston, I tell him he just made a contact with me. We can connect from there. Now, here is where shit gets all fucking weird. Now, I was drinking and shit but I'm not that fucked up yet. Trust me, that comes later. So, while this Black King and I are talking, a Florida Outcast member steps to me and says, "Yo, that's our dude, and he with us" and shit like that. I'm confused. I heard what he said but I don't know why he said it. I address it like, "We're good." It was interrupted by another Florida Outcast bro, who is with the first bro but just turned around and joined into the conversation aggressively. The Black King looks at the Florida Cast bro as confused as I do. The second Florida Cast member posts right up to me and he squares up to me. He's kind of drunk a little and is saying some shit to me in the posture like he is backing the first bro. I'm like, "Are you fucking serious right now, bro? We the same fucking club! Motherfucker, I got your chapter on my back!" I slide my vest off my shoulders to show the bro my Florida soft colors. The first bro sees me removing my vest and takes that as a sign of hostility, as if I were taking my vest off so we can fight bro to bro without getting penalized by our club. "Why you taking your vest off for?" he calls out. I'm aggressively saying what I'm saying, the second bro is saying some response aggressively, and the first bro is asking me repeatedly why I'm taking my vest off in a challenging manner. There is Outcast alpha-male-ism all over the place at this point. So, it appears like we are all about to start brawling in the street. Bros come rushing over to quell the whole situation. They snatch both of us up. I'm pissed off that my bro just came at me, and we are in the same club. I'm more confused than anything, for real. I'm telling him I'm confused. The bros who snatch me up are assuring me that my bro is new, and he's drunk. "I hear all that so why y'all snatching *me* up, then?" is what I'm screaming at them. They are telling me, "The best thing is for y'all to stay separated. So, you go over there."

The shit turned into a big scene of Outcast bros scrambling around to separate the situation. He has a circle of bros talking to him like he is in the wrong. I have Patches, over here with me, telling me that the way I talk sometimes is too aggressive. He has a point, but to me the whole situation was silly. I see the Black King I was talking to in the first place. I talk to him for a little bit more then end it with, "We are good?" He responds, wild-eyed and confused by what he just saw, like, "I thought so! Yeah, we are good. We are good, man!" He slaps hands with me. I'm fucking confused as fuck. So, everyone is still trying to find out what happened and proactively separating us. Bros are coming to their own conclusions about what the fuck happened. Fuck all this.

I slip away from the people who separated me, and I walk over to the Florida bro that I got into it with in the first place. I roll up to him like, "Yo, I don't know what all that shit was, but I ain't came at no one in no sort of way..." He almost immediately interrupts me with a slap of my hand, a hug, and says, "Nah man, that wasn't shit. I thought you was on some other shit, bro. My bad." I tell him I'm mad confused. He says, "Let me buy you a drink, bro." And, that was that. We roll off all fucking hugged up and buying each other drinks for the rest of the night. We talk about the situation at the bar. I think we both are fairly new to the club and are fiery characters off the rip. We both have humble buttons that need to be pressed. We are two live wires plus we are both drinking. The combination is naturally explosive. It always is. Now we both are drunk and give each other ridiculous hugs and shit when we pass by each other. We continually usher each other off to the bar to buy more shots for each other. So at this point, I am fucking hammered. I have no idea how I got back to the clubhouse on my iron.

The rest of the account of the night has all been compiled from speaking to various bros from various chapters, after the fact. So, this is what I got: I came back

135

to the clubhouse and was drinking, chilling and laughing with the bros. Patches said he was going to the hotel. I said I was staying at the clubhouse. Outcast clubhouses don't close. It's not like there is a last call or anything like that. Bros just start falling out on couches, curling up on corners of the floor, and taking refuge on pool tables and shit. So that's what happened, except I decided to pass out in a chair outside with my head in my hands. Solo does a perimeter check to see who is still outside and to close the gate or whatever have you. He sees me and sees that I'm passed out so assumes I'm good. Another bro stumbles outside as well. Solo continues moving, then hears a loud thud. "Oh shit! Yo, Hood!?" I'm down. Solo thought the collapse onto the floor would have woke me but it didn't. He said, "You hit the pavement hard as fuck. No exaggeration." So he and another bro try to carry me inside. I was extra heavy. They put me up, got blankets and I crashed in the clubhouse. That's all she wrote. (Remember JMo from Arizona? Well, years later, he tells me a different account of what happened that night. It involves him and me getting into a fist fight. Neither one of us can remember what we fought over. Neither one of us thinks it matters at this point so we laugh it off, but he says we threw hands at each other, and I snuffed him, and he snuffed me.)

I *can* remember being hung the fuck over in the morning. I drank a beer with my new battle buddy from Florida. We almost beat each other up, became cool, drank until both of us were a mess, and are drinking a beer now, but I never got the bro's name. "What's your name bro?" I ask him. "Ball. Like Oddball," he says. We give each other our final handshakes. I go take a piss and look in the mirror, "Oh shit! What happened to my face?" My eye was swollen, and I had a cut on my nose.

Patches returned to collect me from the clubhouse 'cause he is ready to roll. Three Piece left on his own long ago. It was always his plan. I knew he was going to shake us. It is what it is. He got his cross-country patch. He made the trip as well. He earned it. I think he had an idea of how the trip was going to go, and that got robbed from him by Choppa, so he was not hearing anything that even appeared like it could hinder him. Maybe he had a piece lined up. I'm unsure.

We were rallying up to roll out. Something I like about Patches is when he is ready to move, he moves. When it's time to go, he is ready to go. When it's time for meetings to start, he gets them to start. I like all of that. But no bullshit, this time, I was hurting. I was fucking exhausted. If you think about it and tally it all up, I have been up with very minimal sleep for days. I woke at 6:45 AM from the motel in Colorado and pushed to Cali to arrive at 4:00 AM the next morning, save for an hour nap at a gas station. Then I rested for a couple of hours in the hotel next to the clubhouse. After that I rocked out, partying with Cast until I passed out, which was well into the morning. Now, Patches is here early to hit the road. This is Outcast. I must say, I can perform without much sleep, but what happens is I crash after a few days and need to recharge. I am well into that necessity right now. It is not safe for me to ride. I am still drunk, and I am very tired.

Being an Outcast, I suit up, mount up, and roll out. Patches straps my ruck to the back of his Road King. PT takes point, I fall in the middle, and Patches pulls up the rear. We move out in a tight formation. It's liberating to have no rucksack, no saddlebags, and have my Old Man back on my back. I came here tattered and exhausted as a soldier arriving at the rally point to complete his mission. I am leaving here tattered and exhausted as a biker leaving the California clubhouse to return home. I look like a zombie. I smell like Jack Daniels. I inhale deeply through my nose and smell the blood drying from my cut. I see the California Outcast Chapter spacing away in my mirror. I smile slowly, re-opening the light scab on my lip, and just

137

HOOD LODO

as slowly I raise a middle finger in the air. Fuck you California Chapter. Much love and respect.

Day Seven

We hit the road, and usually there is a bit of heightened awareness necessary when riding in a tight pack. It can be pretty hairy riding that close to other bikes. There is something completely different with how this little group feels. PT is the road captain for the New York chapter, and he is very comfortable in that position. You can feel it. I never rode with this bro before, but when you have people good at what they do, it is a plug and play situation. With Outcast, you realize very quickly that there are different pack leaders with different styles of leading the pack. The pack is a complete unit, and each element in the pack contributes to its dynamic. A simple switch in positioning of two biker elements can change the entire feel of the pack, for better or for worse. A good pack leader has to have almost a supernatural feel for the pack and adjust from there. He dictates the speed and how smoothly transitions happen. He dictates lane changes and when they are necessary. Some pack leaders change lanes sporadically on long trips just to snap the pack out of the zone and keep them alert. Some pack leaders commit to the left lane and push traffic out of the way.

Over time, riding behind PT, I learned his pack leading style. As the number two man, it almost becomes a fluid communication between the pack leader (or point man) and myself. I learn his style to the point that I know what he is going to do before he does it. I know when we pull up on a slower vehicle in a lane and PT decides he is going to push them out of the way, he drops a gear so his pipes are screaming, and he charges the vehicle. He will fall back a few car lengths then zoom right up to the vehicle. As the number two man, I can join in the charge, or let him handle it. He will rev high and charge forward then fall back and charge again. The sound usually alerts the driver to look in their rear view and make the choice to let us go by. If not, then I usually kick down a gear and join in the push. I have learned that PT will hold off for a bit next to a semi-trailer until there is a clearing then accelerate the whole pack by the truck rapidly. This minimizes time in the drag wind of the truck that could blow bikes sideways and into each other, and it lessens time in that proximity vacuum where bikers start to avoid closeness to the truck and lean a little to the left, which is hazardous. There is no space to react to threats in the road, as well, so it's smart to push the pack through that zone rapidly. He does not slinky with rapid accelerations and rapid decreases in speed. There is a consistency in his speed and everything he does. His hand signals are crisp and performed with a preparatory command (blank hand, held high symbolizing a hand gesture is coming), giving all the bikers time to copy the symbol and acknowledge something is coming, then a signal of execution (sharp hand gesture signaling the pack to execute the desired maneuver). It's a discipline, that when done with sharp, crisp movements, passes on a sense of pride in the pack.

The pack feels pride when they look sharp and disciplined. They act how they look. A pack leader dictates that whole feel. If he is lackadaisical with his hand gestures, you will notice a slight lapse in sharpness with the transitions that the pack executes. I noticed, during this trip, how important it is for the pack members to be aware of their immediate relationships in the pack and their duties in those relationships. A member should be able to keep his spacing and speed down to a science. To do this, you have various senses to aid in the whole process. Instead of staring at the bike directly in front of you, have an awareness of that bike. Keep your focus ahead of that bike, so you sense what the bike in front of you is going to do before it does it. You can tell he is going to brake, because the vehicle in front of him did, so you are already preparing for that. You can minimize the slinky shit. If you constantly are checking the mirror of the bike diagonally stacked in front of you and maintaining that picture, it can aid in keeping your spacing. If every time you look at the mirror, his helmet is to the left in the mirror, you accelerate or decelerate to always keep it there. I have a quiet bike, which allows me to hear all the bikes in my immediate relationship to the pack. I can hear when the bike ahead of me is closer than it was before, because the harmonics of the pipes have changed. I try to match whatever that bike is doing by listening and being aware of its rider's actions. If my peripheral sees his left foot do something, I know he just shifted gears. I know up or down depending what we are doing on the road. I am listening to his pipes to confirm these gear shifts as well. Members must be constantly aware of their rear bikers. Sometimes one has to slow down gradually and drift to the side out of the formation, rather than sharply stop in formation and risk your rear bikers locking up their brakes. This prevents the slinky too. All of this awareness helps to keep a tight, safe, pack.

All of these awarenesses are what I am fucking struggling to maintain because I'm fucking exhausted and hung the fuck over. We pull up to a fuel stop, and I zombie walk inside. I can't believe I'm about to do this, but fuck it. I'm hurting right now. I slump on the counter, my right hand grabs the little bottle, and I push it forward. I pay for and walk out with the Five Hour energy shot. I throw it back as if it were a double shot of Jack Daniels. I drank some water and forced myself to eat an egg roll that was rotating slowly on the food warmer. Patches and PT are moving with haste the way I had to on my way to California. I always felt behind the curve, so I was bailing out of gas stations moments after I fueled up, still chewing my food. This was much more deliberate. PT would get a bottle of water at every stop. It wasn't long before I found myself in the same pattern. Staying hydrated is imperative when riding long distance. We would rest and just chill for a moment then use the restroom and push off. Patches comments that we should shorten our time at stops, but he seems very comfortable, chilling, every time we do stop.

There is a sense of security riding with others that you don't get by yourself. It changes everything. If anything were to happen I knew I, at the very worst, had some bros that could ride out and return with whatever I needed. That is a huge relief. Having bros with IDs, I could sleep in motels instead of outside at gas stations or rest stops. They have done it so much, they enjoy a good night in. The tradeoff is this trip back was fucking boring as fuck! The route they took to get to California involved more southern states. So, returning we took the same straight shot back. My route was much different. I hit clubhouses and was scattered all over the northern and midwestern states. They took bland-ass routes like the infamous Route 66.

Route 66, to me, is fucking lame! Every gas station is a cesspool of annoying biker trinkets. Each stop is oversaturated with Route 66 pewter bikes, shot glasses, flasks, belt buckles, mugs, tee shirts, scarves, glasses, thimbles... really! Do people really buy fucking Route 66 thimbles! It is one of the oldest interstates in America, so I guess it's only right to have some old ass bullshit like a fucking Route 66 thimble. Who the fuck walks into a fucking gas station, walks over to that case and is like, "A route 66 thimble! I have been looking all over for one of these! Only twelve dollars? Oh, I'll take two of them, please!"? I don't know. Maybe, if you need to replace that piece in your Monopoly game. I rather be the fucking iron instead of a fucking thimble! No one picks the fucking thimble! You pick the boot or even the fucking top-hat before you pick the fucking thimble. I shake my head and laugh at the idea. Little do I know how important a thimble is to sewing up holes in your leather at this point.

The fucking route is a waste of time. The scenery is the fucking same. You literally are just eating miles of highway. The highway has no character and few variations. You ride through boringness until you get to a tollbooth. Then you roll on through more boringness to the next tollbooth. I have no license plate on my iron. I'm wearing a skull mask and tinted goggles so you know how tollbooths went, right? I slow down, roll up to the window, allow the teller to absorb the skull face, their reflection in my goggles, then blow by. "Hey! Sir?...Excuse me?" Excuse these nuts. Yeah, negative on paying tolls, people. I hate what they stand for, anyway.

One thing I did notice on this route is that there are a whole lot of highway cameras monitoring everything, everywhere. They hang over bridges in black domes. They hang over each lane on overhanging poles. They have low aimed, door-high ones on the side of the road. There are cameras reading license plates. There are cameras, literally, everywhere now. My middle finger got sore from being raised at every one I rode passed. Fuck Big Brother. Patches had asked me, at a rest stop, if the middle fingers were to him. He saw how I would ride by tracing a camera with my arm and middle finger fully extended sometimes standing up on my bike to accentuate my fuck you. So for him to be confused and ask me a silly question like that made me give him a middle finger.

I sobered up a little from the five hours of energy I received from that bottle. It allowed me to absorb all this boringness. At this point though, I'd rather take boringness and stability than rolling by myself, but only because I already did it. I would definitely have loved to roll to Arizona's clubhouse and reconnect with those fucking nutcases, but I left California before them, so I doubt I would have even seen those bros. Furthermore, I am under the command of the pack. I lone-wolfed it already, but now I move where the pack moves. We rolled through Arizona, New Mexico, and Texas. I did not hit any of these states

143

going. I couldn't distinguish one from the other on this boring-ass highway that connects them, so no worries. We keep eating highway at a steady pace. PT pulls off for us to settle in for the night right as night falls. I like this pattern. I do not enjoy riding at night unless I'm in attack mode. Send me on a solo mission, on my quiet bike, with a target, and I become the night. However, riding with bros, with low visibility, dressed all in black, sometimes, is just not as fun (how so much has changed; I appreciate rolling with my bros much more now).

We pull off to some place to eat. All those states have some variation of Mexican food, so we stop and eat at some little burrito shop some ways off the highway. There is desolation in this state. You can feel the joblessness in the air. We order our food and are seated separately but close to each other at the small tables in the joint. A disheveled dude comes in looking like he has not had a home in years. He looks like the stereotypical depiction of a drunkard. He stumbles into the place and hesitates before he gestures if he can sit at the table with me. My instinct is, *What the fuck are you doing, fam? Go sit over there!* He mumbles a greeting to me. I'm sure, simply by his disposition in life, that he is probably ignored or pushed the fuck off everywhere he goes. I allow him to sit down. It is what it is. Right now, he is talking to me, and I am talking back. His English is tolerable, and I soon realize he is telling me jokes. The fucking dude is making me laugh with one-liners. He doesn't bother me for food, he doesn't ask me for money, he just sits down and talks to me outcast to Outcast. I guess the whole situation all just becomes part of this experience.

As we eat, another bum comes in. I'm telling you, I sense that the whole area is dealing with poverty at a level that results in this. The second guy looms around PT. He asks PT for some money or something. PT asks him what he wants the money for and the man says food. PT pulls a portion from his food and says, "Here. Eat this." The man sits down and devours the food PT gave him. He may have nodded in thanks then he took off out the door. Patches laughs, "Shit, I guess the motherfucker was really hungry." We agree as we get up to check in at the motel down the way.

We rumble carefully on the gravel parking lot and find out if there are vacancies. There are. It's a strange setup where there are three beds in a one bedroom living area. As in, one room with a bed that branches off a living-room that has two beds in it. We take it. We walk in the room, and there are three perfectly-made, oversized, homemade cupcakes with frosting and sprinkles on them just sitting on the table. These cupcakes are like fucking six inches in diameter. They were huge and so perfect is was eerie. How long had they been there? That shit threw us the fuck off so bad. PT stops dead in his tracks, stares at the cupcakes and says, "That is straight out of a horror movie." I offload my ruck and claim the single room. I have been running on no battery since states ago. I am ready to sleep. The bed was great to have, although the room reminded me of a military barracks because of the cinder block walls. I can see why the appeal of staying at motels and hotels might trump sleeping on a pool table in a clubhouse sometimes. I knock out on that thought and the fact that PT could not help himself from eating the cupcake. He battled with it. He kept randomly talking about them during his conversation with Patches. Then he ate the fuck out of that horror flick cupcake.

145

HOOD LODO

Day Eight

Morning cracks through the windows. I'm fully rested, and it feels good. Earlier the bros had alerted me that my tail light was out again, so I was going to address that this morning. I was outside on my back under the ass of my bike again. The bulb had completely shattered because I had taped the light in. I never installed the rubber backplate to the light housing. Not a problem, because I had two extra bulbs and the backplate in my tank bag. I used my multi-tool to extract the broken bulb from the connector, installed the bulb into the housing, and sealed it off with the backplate. Now that I could see it in the daylight, as opposed to with a flashlight in my mouth at the clubhouse, I see exactly how it sits and where the wires go and everything, so I fixed it properly. I was not mad at that at all. "Fix it right the first time, so you don't have to fix it again." I'm not sure who in the military used to say that, but it's a simple principle I have learned to appreciate. The light is all set now.

PT woke after eating the horror movie cupcake so Patches attacked the second one. I don't care for pastries and shit, so I didn't indulge. Now, if they had been some complimentary buffalo wings...! I shower up, pack up, suit up, and roll out with the bros. We are back to putting miles down on the pavement, fuel stop to fuel stop, with adequate breaks in between. We are progressing through states at a steady but efficient pace.

We hit a rain storm that was probably the one I dipped through on my way up to California that was supposed to hang around for a week or so. It was significantly worse going through it this time. The rain was beyond upsetting. It completely soaked me from head to toe, and we still were early in the day. It seemed to never

147

end. We rode through this fucking thing for hours. My goggles were useless, because they had water in them, and their fog level was just impossible to deal with. I tried riding with the clear-lensed glasses, but that didn't work either. Ducking down behind my windshield was not working, because I couldn't see through my foggy goggles and the added layer of splashed drops on my windshield. My gloves were soaked, which pisses me off in a unique way. For some reason, I thought these fucking gloves repelled water. No, they don't at all. I don't care how rough you are, and I consider myself pretty rough. I have existed and performed in some horrendous conditions. I pride myself on that ruggedness. But, being miserable for no reason when something as simple as rain gear can prevent it has an extra sting to it right now.

We pull up to a gas stop and people are speaking about how crazy the storm is. They see us and think we are insane. One girl behind the counter says out loud, "Oh, they are bikers they like it. They like the rain." Let me declare something. This biker right here does not like being soaked from head to toe while being cold. He does not like cold rain running down his spine continually. He does not like sloshing boots and heavy gloves. He does not like not being able to see and foggy fuckin goggles. Do not confuse the fact that I *will* ride in those conditions, one hundred times out of one hundred times if I have to, with *liking* it. That would be identical to saying someone who has completed the hot wing challenge at Buffalo Wild wings actually likes having their whole fucking face on fire, their tongue burned, their stomach flamed later, and their asshole converted into an inverted volcano (trust me, I know). No, they handle challenges just to continually push the limit. Patches and PT come fully equipped with rain gear. They both are pulling different versions of waterproof boot covers. I'm sure they had their share of storms that they have pushed through to know they can and will if need be.

148

A memory that I didn't even know was stored in my head until this rain storm got regurgitated. I recall being on a mission in Iraq. I was manning the M2 .50cal machine gun on the gun truck. We halt because there's an IED (Improvised Explosive Device) in the road. Now, once you spot an IED you own that thing, meaning you have to cordon off the area and keep eyes on this fucking thing, so no other friendly forces run into it by accident. You have to call EOD (Explosive Ordinance Disposal) and have them take it from there. IEDs are the main way we get attacked, and they are all over the place at this time. So, needless to say, EOD is spread thin. We were stuck waiting on them, which, sometimes, could be the whole day. I was there frying in the sun when all of a sudden, a cool breeze came ripping through the desert. It went from light to dark in a matter of minutes. Then, it started. It gets 120 degrees in Iraq, easy, with no precipitation. Then, out of fucking nowhere, it starts raining. Let me explain something, and I need you to fully internalize what I'm saying: This is rain like you have never seen in your life! The sky relentlessly pours a flood of water on you, as if it were trying to flush you off the Earth, for days! When I say "days", I mean several fucking *days*. It's biblical! I am stuck in this nonsense. I was probably as resilient as I have ever been in Iraq. *Callous* might even be more accurate, and this relentless pounding of water severely pissed me the fuck off. We were there for, maybe, eleven hours getting hammered by rain. I was hungry too. The gun truck is filled with water from it pouring through the gun turret. There are no trees and the way the rain is coming down nonstop, it's as if you were standing under a cold shower that refused to shut off.

It reminds me that if you can protect yourself from the elements with simple protective wear then do it. It will make all the difference between being dangerously miserable and being able to just endure. Rain gear is mandatory. Fog proof eyewear is mandatory. Perfect gauntlet gloves are mandatory. All of these are items I am learning I need to acquire when I get back. The first thing I do at fuel stops now is go into the bathroom and see if they have air dryers. If they do, I stuff my gloves into the pipe and keep slapping the button. You would be surprised how quickly those things dry shit out. I dry my masks, eyewear, and anything else that I can in order to make the situation bearable. Again, you eventually make it through all storms. It was a relief to get through this one. Even though I was still soaked, eventually curling my body in a certain posture would cut the wind out, and my body heat would warm the water on my skin. I'm wet. We all are wet. We eat up the day and pull into another hotel, hoping they have clothes dryers. We find a dump. They say they have clothes dryers. The price is decent. We are all ready, then they tell us the dryers are broken. We leave.

We are on a divided highway, and we passed several hotels all in proximity to each other so we are on to the next one. In order to get to the hotel we are trying to get to, we have to ride well down the road, find a turnaround point, then come back around to turn around again, then pull into the place. Patches is looking down the street to see where we can turn off. Fuck that, I take the lead and ride out of the parking lot and take a left. Patches and PT follow me. It's a short ride on the sidewalk, and we are where we need to be. We check this place out. It's a go. It has a separate dryer room. We order food, and I'm drying clothes, and all is good. Another day down with good miles. I have no idea what state we are in. I don't care. I am basking in the lack of responsibility right now. It allows me to focus on the ride. It allows me to contrast Patches' riding style with PT's. It allows me to focus on being a pack member. I can't really call this a pack. Outcast runs formations that are hundreds of bikes deep, so to call this a pack is pushing it, but I'm treating it like it is one. It allows me to enjoy another side of being an Outcast, which is having trust in some of my bros. Tomorrow's a new day. I get some sleep.

Day Nine

Another sunrise greets our small group. Our machines are bedded down outside, and they get woken by the sun's rays. We suit up and roll. Today we have intentions of putting down the most miles. We woke up early enough to accomplish this. We hit the road for breakfast. We find a good old-fashioned spot. I get eggs over easy. Patches gets over hard. I never heard of that. What I have learned is an egg is an egg. I really don't give a fuck what form it comes in. I am going to eat it. I order the shit in whatever fashion comes out of my mouth at the time, and Patches just gave me another bullet for that magazine. Now I can randomly say, "Eggs over hard, with corned beef hash and white toast." I order a grapefruit juice, and as we wait on our food, PT and I engage in conversation. We learn about each other's military history. He is a retired Marine. I am still active in the Army Guard. It's inevitable we have a showdown. It's one of the long going rivalries in the armed forces: Army vs. Marines, Navy vs. Air Force. So he goes into his role and says a bunch of cute Marine related bullshit. "We are all you want to be", which I assume is supposed to be a play on "Be all you can be", an outdated Army slogan. He continues with stuff like that. I battle back with him, out of tradition, but I couldn't care less about that rivalry or any of the rivalries, honestly. I have been deployed and have been in the streets, side by side, with every branch. I have had Air Force on missions and Navy with me. I have done countless crap with Marines. The list goes on: Special Ops, civilian contractors, and the likes. The fact of the matter is we are all out there as Americans. It's all one fight. A bullet does not see the slight difference in your uniform pattern. I don't think PT was in the service when there was

153

an active war. It's possible he was. I didn't ask. So, we battle over silly shit like whether or not Marines shoot better. I'm designated marksman trained. He doesn't know what that is and scoffs at the term *marksman* thinking I am saying I am the lowest of the three categories of rifle qualifications we use to score people (marksman, sharp-shooter, expert). Not that he is not knowledgeable, but the DM program was not created by the time he got out of the military. He doesn't know I'm the best shot in my unit. He doesn't know I have consistently been the captain of my unit's rifle team. He doesn't know if you slap a rifle in my hand I'm pretty fucking surgical with it. Honestly, he does not have to in order for us to bond the way we will as Outcast. We battle back and forth. I have heard, but do not retain, cute Marine-relevant phrases. I don't typically entertain this rivalry, and for the few who do challenge me, my experiences kind of shut that down real quick. My specialized training puts the nail in the coffin. He is a proud Marine, and I like that. I am a battle tested proud Army soldier. He likes that. Ultimately, we are servicemen who have taken up arms under that flag of ours. I shake his hand. We laugh. The respect is mutual. In the lives we walk, breaking balls is mandatory. Patches stays out of it. He knows we are bonding. We eat and roll out.

It's an amazing day out. We empty tank after tank, making good time. It looks pretty hopeful that we are going to put down the amount of miles that we had aspired for today. We enter one fuel stop, fuel up, then pull into the parking spaces. Patches looks down at my bike and alerts me that my tire is very low. I look down, and sure as shit it is. I roll out to the air chuck that is on the side of the gas station building. It doesn't work. After scanning my surroundings, I see a tire shop across the road. I rumble my machine over to those dudes to see if they have an air compressor. They direct me into the back of the building. My rear tire is pretty low. Some of the mechanics come out to assist me. One has an air chuck we attach to the airline that another has pulled out for me to use. It doesn't work. His coworker finds another one that does. While filling the tire with air I can hear a disheartening hiss come from the tire. The mechanic spits on his finger and fills the valve on the valve stem with saliva. This is to see if it bubbles indicating air is being lost there. We see nothing. I can hear the air's location. We slowly roll the bike forward and then I see the puncture in my tire. Fuck! The mechanic draws a circle with a grease pencil around the puncture to mark it and tells me to grab some Fix A Flat from Auto Zone down the street. I have heard good and bad things with Fix A Flat. He swears by it and tells me that will "seal that up in no time."

I roll out slowly to my bros to tell them where I am going. Patches is there, but neither of us see PT, so he looks for him while I roll out to Auto Zone. After reading the various cans of Fix A Flat, I purchase a can and fill up my tire. As I'm filling up, I see Patches coming towards me, and he still is not with PT. When he sees what I'm doing, he tells me I just wasted my money. He tells me I need a tire plug. "You talking about a tire patch?" I inquire. "No, it's a plug kit. What aisle did you get that shit in?" We go into Auto Zone and we search the aisles. We find what Patches is talking about. I am staring at the shit confused as I walk out the door with the product. I have never seen this product before. I go out to the bike and rip the package open. I'm ready to give it a try. Patches comes out of Auto Zone and says out loud, "Did you pay for that?" Well, shit, I guess I have to now! I roll back into the store and pay the girl who looks like the last thing she ever wanted to do was ask me to pay for that product she saw me walk out with.

It's all good, little lady. "I don't steal, I rob." Some know exactly what that means. For the rest of you, I will explain this principle right now. Forgive me for this tangent: Yes, both stealing and robbing are taking shit that is not yours. But, there is a slight difference in the motivation behind these two concepts, and that makes all the difference. Stealing is proactive. Robbing is reactive. To steal is to take what is not yours for the selfish reason of desiring, out of greed, something you don't have. It's completely motivated by selfish materialism. It typically leans toward a sneaky, subtle, sly technique. In my opinion, it's a slime-ball, sucker way of moving. It lacks any form of honor. Now, to rob is to take what is not yours as a response to feeling wronged in some form or fashion. There is a motivation other than (but likely containing as well) the desire for the material possession. For example, Robin Hood robbed from the rich, not to have the possessions of the rich, but to provide for those restricted from riches. To rob, sometimes, does not even require keeping the material that was taken if the motivation does not require it. I, personally, have no desire to take what I have not earned. I get more value from working for something, or creating something I need from my own sweat, than taking what someone else has earned. However, if I am restricted from earning what I deserve for reasons that are unjust, I will balance that injustice out with my sweat. That balance might involve a robbery.

I recall attending a music college that eventually got taken over by another collegiate establishment during my sophomore year. In the process, the college made transitions in their tuition policies that ended up severely fucking over many of their enrolled students. Students who were grandfathered under the old tuition rate were unfairly held to purposefully unreasonable scholastic standards specific to them. Which would cause many students to disenroll from the college (without receiving their transcripts). Students would then have to re-enroll at the college's higher tuition rate to continue their education. To me, this was a dishonorable action of stealing from their students. This could not go without some form of retribution. So I took it upon myself to organize a team and rob the fuck out of that college. The college had just been purchased by a new franchise and had changed their name and image. They had several state-of-the-art audio recording studios, and graphic design laboratories. They were focused on recruitment and a positive image. But, again, they wronged their original students by not honoring the tuition rate those students were grandfathered into. My ten-man team hit them in a series of orchestrated robberies, taking thousands of dollars' worth of pro-end audio equipment and computers that pales in comparison to the tuition rate. It was planned and purposeful and meant to cause a bit of chaos to tarnish the image of the school as well. All went flawlessly except for one undisciplined member of the team. One man deviated from the thoroughly planned and executed script and took it upon himself to "disable" one of the cameras in the college during our computer robbery. I laid out exactly what, how, where, and when to do everything for each person, and that was not part of his concern. What he did was stand on a chair and rip what he thought was a power cable out of the camera (it was, rather, the wire that attaches the zooming lens to the body of the camera). He ended up having his face recorded on the camera during this action and subsequently faced criminal charges. Because he deviated from the precise plan, he was the only one charged and had grand larceny over his head. I gave him some equipment and a computer unit to return to the institution to reduce his charge from grand larceny to petty larceny that could be battled out in district court. They settled to some sort of an agreement, and he avoided jail time. He had a stay-away order from the premises. Today the school does not exist, because it got shut down for some more dishonest bullshit it was doing.

In certain contexts, the strategic robbery is better than force, but I'd rather forcefully take your shit. I want to smell you when I fuck you over for your items. I want you to fully understand you are being conquered. I don't even want your bullshit, but I'll take it. Not because it matters to me. But, because it matters to *you*. The fact is, stealing and robbing are illegal. My point is not to highlight the benefits of one over the other or to try and convince you that one is more effective than the other. My point is that I move with a personal code based on values that mean something to me. The law, sometimes, lacks values. So, my code sometimes, supersedes the law. This Auto Zone situation was not one where a robbery was warranted. So, to return to the story: I gladly pay the girl after Patches highlighted my lapse in attention.

I go back out to the bike. Patches guides me. "Damn, you need, like, pliers or some shit." He tells me I have to remove the obstruction. I grab my Gerber (multi-tool) and extend the pliers out of it. I get a grip on the nail. I try to pull it out but the Fix A Flat has oozed out a greasy substance out of the hole onto the nail making it slippery. I try again and pull a one-and-a-half-inch nail out of the tire! "Damn!" Patches exclaims. He has me weave some rubber shit through a stabbing device and fold it back on itself. The idea is to stab this piece of rubber into the hole to plug it then cut the remaining piece off. I do that. I don't really understand how this shit is going to work. I get the concept, but I feel like the use of Fix A Flat and its greasy residue is going to prevent any adhesion. I roll to the convenience store next to Auto Zone to fill the tire with air. Patches goes again to find PT while I ride around the parking lot making sure the plug works. It seems to be holding. Patches returns with PT. After a few more laps around the parking lot we determine I'm ready to hit the highway again. So we hit it, and we hit it hard.

We are still on good pace, but that tire shit kind of has me not feeling too secure. We are riding for a while. I point at Patches while riding, then point down at my rear tire and give him a questioning thumbs up. He pulls up next to me to get a good look. He gives me a thumbs up back. I keep riding. My bike does not feel right. I feel like I'm sliding around. I disregard what Patches tells me shaking my head back and forth and wave myself out of the pack. I pull over to the side of the road. My tire is definitely flat again. What the fuck do I do now? We agree to pull to the next exit to try and formulate a plan. We pull to a gas station, and no one knows where a motorcycle repair or tire store is. I ask pedestrians on the street. No one has any good news for me. PT starts digging in his bike looking for something. A pedestrian I had asked earlier tells me his neighbor, who lives down the street, is always fixing cruisers and he has hoarded a bunch of motorcycle parts, which includes tires. It is a shot in the dark, but I have no other option right now, so I take off with the stranger. We walk to the corner of the gas station, and he points down the street to a white house and tells me his neighbor's name. He wishes me good luck then gets in his car and drives away.

I go back and report the idea to PT and Patches. Patches realized that we never used sealant when we installed the last plug. PT has a different plug system in his saddlebag. We try this thing again using sealant this time. I fill it back up with air then go test ride it to that white house. I see some sexy looking cruisers parked outside. I get off my iron and walk up to the doorway and knock on the door. A lady comes to the door excitedly, until she sees me, then she does that whole speak-through-the-door bullshit. I hate that so much. Your fucking screen door is unlocked, lady. Do you really feel some sort of protection from me with this barrier? You know what screen doors stop? They stop bugs, not me. Anyway, we converse through the door and I run my story down to her. She is asking silly verification questions like, "Where's your bike?" Lady, I asked for your fucking husband. However, I do respect her attempts at a first line of defense. "It's right there, ma'am." I tilt my head down to give her more of a view of the obvious machine behind me. She stalled me

159

enough for some big-ass black dude to come to the door. Ha! This whole time I'm thinking me being black and shit was part of her offishness, but maybe it was simply because I was a stranger knocking on her door in outlaw rags looking for her husband.

Her husband and I speak and then some older guy comes out. We all talk biker shit for a while. That soon leads into military talk, and before you know it we are in full blown socialization mode. Patches comes down the street after a while, and he gets involved in the conversation eventually returning it back to bikes. We end the convo. The dudes give me some extra sealant and vouch for the plug system saying I should be fine with it all the way back to Massachusetts. We will see. The pack takes off and we hit the highway again. Maybe we won't hit the number of miles we want to.

We ride out the day, get some food, and snag a hotel room. If I was not with the pack, I probably would still be stuck trying to figure out what the fuck I was going to do. Maybe I would have ran into some bikers, hours later, who would have informed me about the plug system. Who knows? I'm appreciating the benefits of having a pack. I think the fact that I am on my way home has me wanting to make a few calls. I hit the gas station across the parking lot, buy a six pack of tall boys, and kill them while on the phone outside. I think we all got hit with the same sensation at the same time, because outside I see PT making love to his phone near his bike. We stay in our respective privacy zones. I walk my perimeter. He stays at his post. Patches was on the phone in the room. After my good conversation, I take it upstairs. We put great mileage down today. I have a good pack. I had good beer. Today, I didn't even have to use my AK. I gotta say, it was a good day.

We wake up. Patches is more than ready to pound pavement. He is two stepping all over the place, rubbing his knuckles and ending everything with "yuh know." The energy is crazy. I think everyone is excited in their own way just to be close to the East Coast. He wants to go in for the long haul. He wants to put numbers down the way I put numbers down the last night before rolling into California. I think being hampered by the journey he had with Choppa dropping his bike and the slow pace they had to maintain has caused an itch in him he has to scratch. He wants to attack. We don't bullshit at all hitting the highway. Patches riding style now mimics how he feels. He keeps pushing the pack by riding up next to me then falling back. I don't budge, and I maintain my distance from PT. There are points when Patches flies damn almost past me then falls back in position. He is not looking at me or signaling PT to push forward; I think he is just wanting to attack something.

We keep pushing. We have our patterns pretty much down solid. PT knows how much he can push my bike before I really need fuel, and he stretches my tank. This is another luxury of rolling with extra fuel and a pack. The weather is fair. After that major storm we rolled through, both Patches and PT are wearing their rain gear. I'm the only one with The Old Man out. Our all black uniform and the way we ride tight makes it undeniable that we are all represented by my rags. My rags grab attention especially with the duster. They just do.

I was parked outside a fuel shop waiting for PT and Patches to finish fueling when a dude walking up from behind me addresses me, "I like your cut." "What?" I say. He repeats himself, "I like your cut. You know, your rags. I'm a biker too." I'm just staring at this guy. He has stopped at a respectful distance from me. I'm looking at him from over my shoulder, so I suggest with a hand gesture for him to stand in front of me. He does and continues, "Yeah I got my cut in the car, man." He introduces himself as the regional vice president of his club. He says he's from Massachusetts. I have never heard

161

of his club. He commences to tell me they have 131 chapters and they are based out of Boston. "Where?" I ask. He says his mother chapter is out of Dorchester. "Really, where?" I was born and raised in Dorchester. I ask him how long his club has been around. He says since 1969. Interesting, that's how long Outcast has been in existence. He tells me how they have members of all walks of life and how they accept everyone. "You know, man, we just ride man, and you know we keep to ourselves, but we don't take no shit..." He goes on about some of his members getting into it with the OLs (Outlaws MC) recently and how he is waiting on the call from the president. He is rambling with pseudo-confidence, "I haven't heard from him yet, man. I'm not with all that shit, man. We can talk or meet up and it's whatever. But I have not heard from..." He drops the wrong name of the Massachusetts Outlaws president. I call him out on it. He says, "Well, uh, I don't really know those dudes, man. But, I mean, he just needs to call me, you know?"

I'm listening to this guy kind of amused. I continue questioning him, "How long have you been in the club?" I ask. "Three years. We used to have (insignificant name) as president, but then I took over. New management. I love the guy but..." He rambles on some more. It's as if he is peacocking for my approval or something. Patches and PT are ear hustling the conversation. PT does not look amused by this dude at all, but he is digging how I am handling it. I think he is trying, to no avail, to network somehow. I'm not feeling his energy though. It feels fake. He continues expressing how valid his club is. He explains all the changes in patches they have had and shows me a picture on his phone of when they used to wear "Mass" as a bottom rocker. Wearing "Mass" to some degree technically is not claiming a territory as we do by wearing the full state name of "Massachusetts". I think they might have caught flak for that, so they changed it. He speaks of the new colors. I tell him to go get them. While he is gone, I explain

162

to Patches what is happening. I really am just letting the man talk. I'm not trying to prove anything. I'm genuinely trying to have a good vibe from the man but it's just resulting in oddness. He comes back with his rags, and I advise him that he should just familiarize himself with some of the big names in his community. Trying to name drop the OLs and getting the name wrong bothers me. It shows me that you are trying to validate yourself as being a factor in our tier of the motorcycle community when you are not. He holds up his rags for me. I tell him to stand with it for a while; I am going to take a picture. "Cool man, yeah man." I take the picture of his full body and rags. He continues, "Can I take a picture with you guys, man?" I respond, "No. I don't do pictures. He might let you." I look at Patches knowing he is going to fall exactly in suit with what I just said. "I don't have my shit on," he says. I continue, "Yeah. No." He is glad he made a contact. I take his number and tell him I will pick up with him from there. He asks if he can come down with his members to the clubhouse. "We will get to all of that," is what I say to him. Truth is, if he thinks that meeting me in a parking lot and having the exchange we just had is going to allow him or his club to rub elbows with mine is absolutely wrong. Nothing he expressed while having my attention was actually about him as a person. It was all about him as whatever persona he is projecting as a biker and none of that shit landed with me. We shake hands and he goes on his way. Once I send the name, phone number, and picture to the club we will know exactly who and what his club is all about. Fullback will do that in ten minutes. No worries.

We mount up and roll out. We attack the highway harder and harder. As we get closer to the East Coast the feel on the road gradually changes. The East Coast is vicious. You can feel it on the road, especially when you come from across the whole country. It's an east coast energy that is just *icy* all the time for no apparent reason.

163

HOOD LODO

It's as if every person on the road is in a frantic hurry to go nowhere fast. There is a lack of patience and a general disrespect you can feel. I don't have road rage or anything but people who have no regard for motorcycles drives me up the pole. I am starting to observe some of this disrespect and it's changing my mood. The whole "they are not going to get in front of me" attitude that primes one to do some bold bullshit on the road results in us motorcyclists risking severe injury or death.

It's that simple. We are the vulnerable ones out here. You really don't embrace it until you ride. You view the road in a whole different way. Fatality is around every corner and in every direction. You can slam on your brakes in a car, and all four wheels attempt to stop you as you slide all over the place. Slam your brakes on a motorcycle, and your wheels will slide out from under you, and you will go down. You can run over road kill in a car and complain how fucking gross that was. Hit roadkill on a motorcycle, and you go down. You can turn on an off-ramp a little too fast 'cause you were answering a text in your car. You hit an off-ramp a little too fast on a motorcycle or lean too much into that turn, and goodbye. You can drink and drive multiple times and laugh about it like, "I was so fucking hammered..." bla bla bla. Despite the fact that a lot of bros do drink, we generally do respect very deeply that alcohol and motorcycles is a match made in hell. There is no way around that fact. You suck on a bike drunk. You just do. You will eventually go down, and hopefully you can recover. Motorcycles do not forgive. A good club looks very hard after each other in this respect. If you run over black ice, sand, gravel, oil or the likes, you slide in a car. Hit any of that on a bike at the wrong speed or angle, and you go down. Fender benders are common in cars. You get fender tapped on a bike, and you are going to the hospital. We bikers know the risk we choose being on a motorcycle, and we pride ourselves in taking safety courses and looking out for each other with tight formations and

164

what not. It still does not remove the fact that we get penalized for someone else's mistakes each time. A motorcycle against anything and the motorcycle loses. You hit a deer, and your insurance gets a call. We hit a deer, and it's ballgame. Someone runs a red light in a car, and they might get fucked up while the other car is fine. That might be justice. Someone runs a red light, and no matter what, the biker gets fucked up. For this reason, bikers are very sensitive to people, and other bikers, being dickheads on the road. It is what it is. Something I have noticed is that drivers treat single riders, or even a mob of unorganized riders popping stunts, differently than they treat an organized formation of bikes. This is just fact. I'm not saying riders need to ride like Outcast. I'm just saying that there is less of a respect level when you don't. Because of this shared risk, there is a common respect for all members of the two-wheeled family amongst each other.

I'm getting contacts pretty much at each fuel point on the East Coast from assorted MC members that introduce themselves to me after they view it cool to do so. Networking, at this point, is not a bad thing. So I do it. There is method behind that madness but that's Outcast business. We fuel up and hit the pavement. It's getting into nighttime. I'm in familiar states but have not hit Massachusetts yet. We are nearing the point where PT is going to break off and it's going to be the Mass Cast duo. I make a comment to Patches about not wearing his vest since it's not raining. He thinks about it, half smirks, and says, "Shit, I'm gon' put that motherfucker on for you right now, man. Yuh know." He throws The Old Man on, and you can see our prided emblem on his back for exactly three seconds before The Old Man gets smothered by Patches' long ass grey and black dreads. We fuel up at our final fuel stop as a pack. PT makes sure he has my number and tells me he will ride with me anytime. For some reason I think words like that don't come out of this man's mouth

165

often, so I am honored. I give him his respects. I feel the same way. He's a good point man. Him and Patches have a final confirmation of a conversation we had earlier concerning the north east chapters connecting soon. We mount up and roll out for the final leg of the trek.

Our formation is solid. I know PT does not like riding at night, so he might take it in somewhere, but Patches and I are pushing. We have a lot of miles to put down and we could stop, but I don't think Patches is going to. He is finally getting to scratch that itch. We ride for what seems like forever, then PT breaks off in Jersey. Soon as he breaks off, Patches fucking opens up! I mean this motherfucker opens up! We are flying all over the fucking place. Usually, I would be more than pleased ripping up the highway with Patches. My attitude is weird though. I'm so close to home; I do not want to get snagged by east coast cops. Fuck no! I will get reamed with everything in the book if I do. So I'm playing it cool. I'm keeping with him, but he is fucking all over the place! My man is flying in and out of lanes. We ride the breakdown lane more than anything because of traffic and bullshit, but as soon as it opens up we are back to braiding the highway up. He's dipping in and out of cars. I dip my way. Then, we rejoin. It felt good. I just was not about the bullshit, so there are times I would fall way back. It was all good though. At one point, I lost eyes on him and was ahead of him so pulled over. He pulled up and asked me, "Why is your bike smoking?" I looked down and saw steam billowing from a run off hose. I thought it was the coolant run-off hose. No big deal. We take back off ripping up the highway.

I can smell my state in the air. It still is hours before I get to her. I can almost taste my welcome home drink on my tongue. Hours pass by burning up I-95 when that "Welcome to Massachusetts" sign shows its face. As I cross into my state, success hits me. It's official. I take a deep inhalation. I lift my chin up in the wind. I raise my middle finger up into the sky...

166

X-Ray, this is Hood Lodo. I say again, this is Hood Lodo. RP reached. 1 victor, 1 pack. Time: now, how copy? Mission Cross Country completed. Hood Lodo out.

HOOD LODO

Epilogue

After traveling from ocean to ocean, there is a liberating realization that there is literally nowhere in the United States in which I cannot pop up. I felt like the entire country was my backyard. This set a real early standard and tone for how my Outcast career was going to continue to unfold. Because I travelled the whole span of the country, every other trip was not as difficult. Much of it all comes down to mental toughness, as opposed to anything else. I recall being at church, after I got back from my trip, and Fullback jokingly making the comment, "Now he's going to think he's all that." I also recall Grass saying, "Many times people make a trip like that, then they don't ride again for years." Little did they know how wrong they both were. It had the opposite effect on me. I rode, and ride everywhere, because I feel limitless. I don't have a windshield, radio, not even real saddlebags on my V-Rod Muscle. Honestly, after losing all your gear in a saddlebag while in the initial state of a cross-country trip, and still making it, you know you can do it again if you had to with nothing. I wear whatever I am wearing, and I will take off to show up in some far-away state the next day. I "scumbag" everywhere, because that was the tone set from the cross-country trip. Now, for better or for worse, my motto is "Anywhere, anytime, unannounced," and that is how I ride. The roots of a true Scumbag, Road Warrior, minimalist are what have been planted, and what a beast of a tree have those roots grown to become.

A true Outcast has no self-set limitation to his mind, his body, or his soul. He will battle personally to condition each of those. Each time he rides his motorcycle, he is faced with individual challenges that condition his mind, his body, or his soul. Each time he performs maintenance on his iron, even if he doesn't want to, he conditions his mind to embrace that he must do certain things because it's his duty. Each time he pushes another mile on his iron in horrendous weather, because he knows his brother is waiting for him, he is conditioning his body to know that it can take much more than he thinks; Pain is weakness leaving the body. Each time a member goes through his individual ritual right before he mounts his iron, and the rumble from his engine fills the air, he is conditioning his soul to understand that the commitment to this one ride is a commitment to this whole life.

As each individual member does the same, the mind body and soul of The Old Man as a collective get conditioned as well. As the collective mind becomes strong and focused, it conditions out the weakness created by negativity and frivolous shit that challenges the organization. As the collective body moves together as one and continually makes a unified presence across the nation, it conditions itself to create a standard of strength based on the fact that we are most powerful together. Because we are powerful when we, as individuals, are alone. Always be powerful.

Most importantly, as each individual member grows his mind by riding and learning about this nation and the bros present and gone, as he rides and has experiences that challenge his body to perform in the name of Outcast, whether that be to donate blood or to draw blood, as he gets mentally tough and physically durable to scumbag wherever for whatever in the name of Outcast, it creates in that individual an Outcast *spirit*. It's a spirit that generates confidence and power because it is rooted from experience. Continually make experiences, and you will make confidence, which makes power. This is because you will know from experiences what you are talking about.

Experiences all start with riding your shit. Make being on your iron a movement. As the individual harnesses and polishes his Outcast spirit, so too does the

170

collection of individual spirits create and epitomize the total soul of The Old Man. We are him because he is us. So when we carry on, we are carrying on a history that we are creating. Now create and share your history. Outcast! Outcast! Outcast!

Made in the USA
Middletown, DE
23 October 2018